SQUIRMS TO LEARN:
If You're Not Squirming, You're Not Learning!

Dawn

Best Wishes,
Keep on
Squirming!

Jeff

Squirm To Learn

Business/Leadership/Inspiration/Self Help

**Library of Congress
Cataloging-in-Publication Data TXu 922-770**

Magee, Jeffrey L. Ph.D., PDM, CSP, CMC
Simons, Dave
Simons, Ginny
Squirm To Learn: If You're Not Squirming, You're Not Learning!

Cecil, Meghan, editor
Hannesson, Robb, project manager
Jurgensen, Tim, book cover design
Litt, Amie, layout and design
Simons, Mike, photographer

No portion of this book can be used in any manner without the written permission of the authors or publisher.

© 2002 by, Jeffrey L. Magee, Ph.D., PDM, CSP, CMC
Dave Simons, Ginny Simons

For information regarding special discounts for bulk purchases for business training immersion, large groups, families and gifts, please contact the following:

P.O. Box 701918
Tulsa, OK 74170-1918
Toll free 1-877-90-MAGEE or
1-800-532-0082
ISBN: 0-9718010-1-0

SQUIRM to LEARN: If You're Not Squirming, You're Not Learning!

By The **Squirmologist** Team Of:

Dave Simons

Jeffrey Magee, Ph.D., PDM, CSP, CMC

Ginny Simons

SQUIRM To LEARN
ISBN # 0-9718010-1-0
US $12.95
Copyright 2002

Table of Contents

Introduction	A Squirm Is Born	7
Chapter One	A Problem at The Company	13
Chapter Two	The Story of Squirm	29
Chapter Three	The Great Divide	37
Chapter Four	A Hidden Traitor	45
Chapter Five	The Excuse Factory	53
Chapter Six	The Town of Squelch	57
Chapter Seven	The Family That Complains Together, Remains Together	67
Chapter Eight	A Strange Phenomenon	73
Chapter Nine	A Paradoxical Conundrum	75

Chapter Ten	Why The Whinery Wasn't Working	79
Chapter Eleven	The Secret Meeting	85
Chapter Twelve	Stew Starts to Stew	91
Chapter Thirteen	Wanta And The Professor	99
Chapter Fourteen	Making It Happen	103
About The Authors	Simons, Magee, Simons	115

Introduction
A Squirm Is Born

It was a slightly overcast morning as we headed down the turnpike from Tulsa to the town of Stroud, Oklahoma, on our way to the monthly meeting of our chapter of the National Speaker's Association. We always look forward to these Oklahoma Speakers Association meetings. They're a great place to learn and connect with others who possess the same passion for their respective professions as we do for ours.

Unbeknownst to us, this meeting would be different from the others we had attended, not because of the topic, but because of the result. The featured presenter was a well-known trainer and television celebrity from the Dallas, Texas area named Nikki McCuistion. Nikki's interactive style is one that we personally use in our training, and one with which we are comfortable as trainers as well as a participants.

Needless to say, we interacted with Nikki during her session. In our banter back and forth she asked us questions and moved us into our "learning zone." When she did this she pointed out, in front of everyone present, "I'm making you squirm, aren't I? You know, that's my job, don't you? If you don't squirm a little, you're really not learning much."

After the meeting, as we all visited, one of us engaged in one-on-one dialogue with her.

Dave thanked her for the program she had presented. She proudly grinned at him and said, "You squirmed! You did. I gotcha!" He agreed and thanked her for being strong enough and bold enough to have that affect on him, and on a number of others who were willing to squirm. Pondering the morning's lessons on the way back to Tulsa, it hit him. LIGHT BULB!— Squirm.

The illumination from that bulb came to be when we got together after that meeting and started discussing the squirming concept and we recognized – Squirm to Learn.

Much has been written recently about cheese and fish in dozens of other books, all with creative metaphors, and they all deal with the topic of *change*. But what occurred to all of us, who have collaborated on this project, is that *the real issue is not change…or resistance to it.* **The real issue is resistance to learning.**

Learning can cause each of us to challenge our beliefs and threaten what we now already know.

Far too many resist the learning. Learning always precedes change. After all, if you haven't learned what, or how, or why, then you cannot change. Change is relatively easy, if the learning has taken place.

All of us who have collaborated on this effort are professional trainers-authors-Keynoters, and have personally encountered this resistance to learning so many people have and even protect. The sheer unwillingness to learn something new because of the threat to one's current personal knowledge makes change impossible, and growth as well.

What was most mysterious about this revelation was *where* this light bulb experience occurred. Stroud Oklahoma!

Stroud is a small town nestled comfortably next to the Turner Turnpike on Interstate 44. This is the main highway between Tulsa and Oklahoma City, and Stroud is the midpoint. It is convenient that the monthly NSA-OK meetings are held in Stroud, since it's the same amount of driving for both sides of the state. Stroud, I should also point out, is about the ONLY thing on that stretch of road, save for a couple of toll plazas.

The small town managed to capitalize on its location and successfully attracted a large outlet mall to locate there. It became a significant employer in the area by the late 1980's.

However, the horrible tornadoes that hit the Oklahoma City area in the spring of 1999 moved in a northeasterly direction and as luck would have it, drew a bead on Stroud. The storm completely leveled the mall and thus destroyed one of the town's largest resources.

But the town of Stroud was not destroyed. The hearts and minds of the "Stroudians" were determined to overcome this tragic event. They dug in and managed to survive.

As the town looked for new industries and means of growing, it has learned to make the best of a bad situation. We've no doubt that the town to which you are about to be introduced, in many respects, resembles Stroud.

Perhaps the next time you happen to be traveling on Interstate 44 you'll stop in Stroud and take a leisurely drive through the downtown area.

Be sure to stop at the diner for a great burger and try some barbecue at one of the local smokehouses. Main Street Stroud is historic Route 66, and it's worth the diversion of just saying you have driven that road. If you'll drive slowly, look closely, and listen, you just might see and hear some Squirming going on.

Chapter One:
A Problem at The Company

The financial news of the day was grim. The market was down again due to earnings reports that did not meet expectations. Compounding the problem were further news of downsizing, corporate mergers that seemed threatening to investors and employees alike, misleading financial statements, unethical leaders, complacent colleagues, and a host of other alarming reports that might cause a person to want to become a hermit.

In the midst of all of this doom and gloom, there was a ray of sunshine and hope. The Company, founded by J. T. Hoopes, who was still at the helm, had a long-standing tradition of going against the current trends. J. T., the developer of an innovative line of products that served a wide variety of businesses, was a unique individual. His keen insights and no-nonsense approach to accountability, coupled with his true concern for people -- employees, customers, vendors, and the community -- helped him forge a level of success in business equaled by few but rivaled by many. His uncompromising honesty, integrity, and ethics helped him forge a business success story that to this day is the object of intense study. Tales of his exploits were legendary. He was one of the most admired business leaders of his generation, and served as a role model for many budding entrepreneurs who sought to imitate his success.

The Company made its home on a vast expanse of land comfortably situated near The City. Nestled in the rolling hills south of The City, amid lush, green grassy areas, wooded coves, and flower gardens, the atmosphere felt more like a vacation resort than a leading corporate business giant.

Within The Company's corporate compound, situated comfortably in the middle of the offices and the various flora, was a special building. It was the one in which J. T. took the most pride and satisfaction and the one he believed was the most important not only to the people but also to The Company. It was known simply as The Learning Zone. This unique place was the reason The Company stood out and retained its leadership role in the ever-changing business climate. The Learning Zone was unique, but it was also frightening. Everyone knew that when you entered The Learning Zone, you were leaving The Comfort Zone behind. It was the place where many a stellar career had begun. J. T. believed that to learn, to really enter The Learning Zone, one must leave The Comfort Zone behind.

J. T. Hoopes believed that continuous learning was so important -- the essence of life -- that he built an entire corporate culture around that principle. He was never personally content with what he already knew and was on a constant search for new knowledge. His most often used word was, *Why?* He asked that a lot. He was always seeking to know beyond what he already knew. He considered himself to be a lifelong learner and only associated with those who were of the same mindset.

The appearance and physical structure of the Learning Zone were nothing special. It was a big, square brick building that sat right in the middle of everything. Standing three stories tall, the nondescript outside of the Learning Zone in no way reflected the awesome power of what happened inside of it. It was truly the closest thing to a magical place that existed in corporate America, or the entire business world for that matter.

Almost every one of The Company's employees had a story to tell about The Learning Zone and most of those stories revolved around the person's first visit there. Employees of The Company all described their initial visit to The Learning Zone in terms of the fear they felt as they entered and the awesome, exhilarating feelings that they felt when they left. Each person admitted that they had never been the same since. Everyone knew that The Learning Zone intended to change people through the learning experience. They also understood, thanks to J. T., that all learning experiences involved some level of discomfort in adults. He prepared them for that, taught them it was okay to actually like it.

A large sign mounted over the main entrance to the Learning Zone had only three words written on it. In bright red letters, it read, Prepare to SQUIRM! Everyone knew what it meant.

Very few people new to The Company looked forward to their first visit to the Learning Zone, but usually after several trips, they began to look forward to their learning sessions. It was a joy for J. T. to watch people feel great about themselves as they remembered how to learn again. They said they felt liberated as they re-discovered their lost ability, the joy of discovering and learning new things, and the extreme pride they felt once they changed as a result of their learning. Many said it made them feel years younger. Even young people said that!

J.T. believed that if you were not learning continuously you became stagnant, and stagnancy made you feel old. Even at his ripe old age of 75 (which surprised most people), he had more zest and energy than many people one third of his age. He attributed these things to his desire, his passion, to learn. He confided in many of his closest colleagues that he considered himself a "learning evangelist."

J. T. was often interviewed and asked how he became so adamant about learning. He loved to answer that question. "Look at little children, infants," he would say. "Watch the joy on their faces as they learn and discover something new. They are so proud of themselves, and the ones who love them are proud of them as well. Where do you think their boundless energy comes from? Learning, that's where! Every day is a new adventure. They can hardly wait for the new day to dawn. Why? It's so their excitement of discovery -- of learning -- can once again fully energize and captivate them. In fact, just try to stop a youngster from learning. Aside from the fact that it's practically impossible, it would be abusive!"

Then J.T. would become a bit somber. "But, what happens when they begin growing older?" He would frown. "What happens is that other's attempts to *squelch* their learning begin to take root. Oh, it's not intentional, mind you. It just happens. Mostly by well-meaning adults -- teachers, parents, siblings -- who start defining what should be learned, what's stupid, what's not, and so on. Even simple little phrases like 'don't be so nosey,' 'that's a stupid question,' 'you sure do ask a lot of questions,' repeated often enough over time, start the *squelching* process.

"As time passes, much curiosity and creativity is lost, and with it the desire to learn. Every time the learning desire is *squelched*, a little bit of something inside the person dies. That's why there are so many people living unfulfilled and unhappy lives. They are not *living* life, they are merely *surviving* in a lifeless existence. What I have always tried to do is give back to people what they have lost. That is their joy of living. That joy comes from learning, from growing and changing, not from merely surviving in a state of stagnancy."

J. T. would usually be on a roll by this point. Rarely would you see him as worked-up as when he was expounding on this topic of learning. He could go on for hours, and often did.

"If you're learning, you're living," he was fond of saying. "If you stop learning, part of you dies. Only it's a slow death. Now, I ask you, does that sound appealing? Absolutely not! But you then have to wonder, why do so many people choose it?

Slow death chosen over learning and change. That's a mind blower!"

J. T. frequently talked about goals, but when he spoke the word "goals," everyone knew it was an acronym. He sometimes even pronounced it as "G-O-A-L-S." Those associated with him knew what it stood for: **G**o **O**utside **A**nd **L**eave **S**ecurity. Outside, of course, meant out of your personal comfort zone; and security referred to the fear of change that resists learning.

"Learning involves opening one's mind to new possibilities and ideas and challenging the knowledge one currently possesses, which is often obsolete. Everyone talks about change, and resistance to change, but they're missing the real point…LEARNING! If you're learning, you have no choice but to change. If you don't want to change, what should you do? Stop learning! The one constant in life is change, and it takes learning new things to help one adapt to that change. Without continuous learning, you might as well be dead."

J.T.'s company had become legendary for its training programs. On any given day, one could attend courses on every skill imaginable. J. T. encouraged his people to participate and most of the learning programs were voluntary. At least one program per week, however, was required. Over time the company established a habit of learning.

Frequently, J. T. would visit some of these learning activities in The Learning Zone. He would randomly show up just to let people know how serious he was. Also, he always participated. He set the example and was quick to point out that he learned something new at every session he attended, no matter how basic it was and how many times he had attended it. "With an open mind," he said, "and a desire to learn, there is always something new to be discovered. You just have to be committed to discovering it."

As he popped in to the Lunch and Learn Seminar one Friday, he was upset to see the lack of attentiveness of some people in attendance. This particular Friday program was an essential one, and he expected people to vigorously and enthusiastically participate. He was appalled to find several people showing such a strong disinterest in the session. Chief among them was one of his managers, Andy Pathy. Andy was a person who J. T. had personally recruited to join his team, and Andy had been excited to come on board.

What J. T. saw in Andy then reminded him of himself many years earlier. Bright, eager, passionate about life, and with a very strong character, Andy had seemed like one of a handful of people who held the key to the continued leadership of J. T.'s enterprise. However, what J. T. saw during this learning session was, to put it mildly, extremely disheartening. J. T.'s disappointment was apparent to the most casual observer.

Andy was acting as if being in the session was punishment. It was rather obvious that he did not notice J. T.'s presence in the back of the room. Andy was being confrontational, rude, and disruptive. He frequently challenged the instructor, and became extremely defensive when a question was asked of him. His entire demeanor was saying, *What can YOU possibly teach ME?* He acted like he knew it all, and J. T. knew that if a person felt he knew it all, then he couldn't know any more. In J. T.'s opinion, Andy was derailing the entire session. Any time Andy came close to the point of *squirming*, he became very agitated and extremely negative. It was easy for J. T. to see how one person's negative energy was draining the life and spirit out of everyone in the room. His attitude was *squelching* the learning that should have been taking place.

Of even greater concern was the message that this behavior was sending to the other employees of

The Company. Above all, J. T. expected his managers to set an example for others to follow. He had personally done that, still did, and considered it the responsibility of every manager in the entire organization. Andy was acting like a know-it-all, and to J. T., know-it-alls were know-it-nots.

As was his usual habit, J. T. did not allow this behavior to go unnoticed and he addressed it swiftly and efficiently. He asked his assistant to schedule a meeting that very afternoon with Andy. The meeting was set for 3:30.

J. T. met Andy in his lobby area and cordially invited him into his office. After a brief exchange of pleasantries, he asked Andy how he believed things were going for him. Andy, true to his nature, explained that he had gotten the job down cold, felt he was doing it well, and for all intents and purposes had made no mistakes. He also stressed how busy he was, and how all of this additional learning was interfering with his work schedule. "I just don't have time for it," he said.
Andy went on to point out how all this "new" learning was causing people to question the way things were being done, and even his way of doing things. "It seems to create a lot of chaos," he explained, "and we tend to be less efficient when

things get chaotic. The unpredictability can be very frustrating."

That's when J. T. chimed in. "You know, Andy, I've always encouraged our employees to be lifelong learners. I've tried to be an example of that. Always asking why. Always trying something new, always trying to stretch. That's what has made this company what it is today, and that is the way it must be for us to continue our leadership. As I watched you in that learning session today, I could not believe how you behaved. You were being a *derailer*." That was a term that Andy had heard J. T use before, but did not fully understand.

"The problem, I believe, is that you are afraid of *squirming* -- you know, that uncomfortable feeling you get when you have to combine learning with change and move outside your Comfort Zone. Do you think I might be right?"

Andy was shocked to hear J. T. describe him this way. He always saw himself as a dedicated, hard worker, and his initial urge was to argue and defend himself. Before he did, he caught himself and reflected on what had just been said. Could it be? He was about to react in the exact way he denied he acted. Instead, he thought for a moment and realized that what J. T. was describing was perhaps more true than he cared to admit. He thought a moment longer and then hesitantly agreed. "Yes, I guess in a way you might be right. It never was my intention, just my reaction. It just seems like we are always in the lead, and I constantly ask myself, *Why change? We've got it. Let's keep it the way it is. We're on top, why fool with that?*"

"There's that Comfort Zone, Andy," J. T. pointed out. "Peter Drucker once said, 'The best way to predict the future is to create it.' And that is the reason I am so adamant about learning. The future is coming, Andy, and you cannot stop it. No one can. It's absurd to even think you can. That's crazy thinking; it's not even thinking at all! The world is changing and changing fast. If we are not leading the change, then we will ultimately be following those who are. Who wants to be a follower? Do you?"

Andy shook his head to let J. T. know he had no desire to be a follower.

"If we are not continuously learning and changing, we will ultimately become followers. The only way to grow is to change, and the only way to change is to learn. Andy, I need you to be leading these learning initiatives, not stifling them. See those two trees out on the lawn?" J. T. pointed to a window in his office. One tree was barren, the other lush with leaves and flowers in full bloom. "Do you know the difference between them? One is living, and the other is dead. The one that is living is growing, and changing -- daily, in fact. The other does not change. It has looked that way for several years. Even during the winter, when they both may look the same, the living tree is still growing, still changing. The dead one never changes. And that's what learning accomplishes. If we are like the living tree, we will continue to grow, continue to change. Otherwise we are like the dead tree. We don't change. There is a difference between dormant and dead. Does that make sense?"

J. T. continued, "We all seek a life that has meaning, and knowledge provides the catalyst for that meaning. Without knowledge, our options are limited at best, at worst nonexistent. You must learn -- there's no getting past it, if you want to be happy in this life."

Andy nodded in understanding. As he tried to recall the new things he had learned in the past several years, it dawned on him that he had not really pursued any new knowledge. In fact, as he thought about it, he realized that he had been somewhat resistant to learning. He defended what he knew rather than question it. Specific learning opportunities had presented themselves over the years, but he had argued against them vigorously. As he struggled to remember why he was so resistant, the reasons made almost no sense. They were foolish, just a bunch of lame excuses that he recognized as such. Suddenly he realized that he was indeed stuck in his Comfort Zone, and learning threatened to move him into the no man's land of uncertainty. All of a sudden, that didn't seem like such a bad idea.

"When I was young, like you Andy, and new in business," J. T. said, "I could have settled for doing things the way they had always been done. In fact, at times, that seemed like a very attractive option. Changing things is not an easy task, particularly people's minds and attitudes. But something inside me caused me to always want to know more. People thought I was crazy. 'Leave it alone,' they'd say. 'We've always done it this way, or that way, why can't you leave well enough alone?' Everyday, that's the kind of thing I'd hear, and it can start wearing on you. Tough as it was, I refused to listen. I made up my own mind; I didn't let others make it up for me. After all, I'm the one in charge of what I believe. So I pressed onward. I wanted to learn *Why?* and I did. In the process, our company developed a whole new way of doing business. As a matter of fact, people began thinking J. T. stood for *Jump Through Hoops*. I thought it was funny, but they were serious."

J. T. knew he had caught Andy's attention. "Oddly enough, all of those *squelchers* slowly started coming around. It wasn't fast, mind you, but one-by-one, they began *squirming*. Persistence paid off. Persistence, what a missing ingredient in most people today," J. T. reflected. "Everyone wants instant success. But it can't happen without persistence, and certainly in the area of learning which requires a lot of it."

Andy wanted to know, "How did you keep that drive to learn, to know? Seems like I get caught up in thinking that I already know certain things, and I stop feeling the need to learn. Then I hear the voices of other people telling me to slow down, ease up. They're *squelchers*, I think you call them. Unfortunately, I start listening to them and I cave in to the pressure. I guess that's when I start becoming resistant to accepting new ideas. I give in to too many negative voices shouting at me. Where did you learn to learn and not listen to all of that negative chatter?"

"I've thought about that often," J. T. said. "I guess I'm different in that way, not because I'm any smarter or better than anyone else. It's just that learning has been ingrained in me since when I was a young boy. My parents used to tell me a story when I was little. It was my favorite. The way they told it made it seem so real, so alive, that I came to believe it was more than just a story. I feel like I am actually living that fairy tale. Whenever they'd ask if I'd like a story, I always asked them to tell me the same one. I've told it to my children and grandchildren and to my employees as well. It's the Story of Squirm. Would you like to hear it?"

Andy had heard that J. T. was a legendary storyteller. He had also heard his colleagues speak of the Story of Squirm and he relished the opportunity to hear this great man share something so personally important to him.

"I would be honored if you would share it with me," Andy said.

J. T. was pleased at Andy's genuine interest. He began, "Once upon a time, in a town not far away from yours…"

Chapter Two:
The Story of Squirm

Once upon a time, in a town not far away from yours, was a place considered by many to be the greatest place in the world, the town of Squirm. It was very much like your town in many ways, but also very different. The joy of living, the zest for life, was something one would feel everywhere they went in Squirm. There was no place on earth quite like it. Squirm was not only a place, it was an attitude, and it defined the townspeople and their life in this grand land.

Our story begins on a bright, sunny day in the town of Squirm. It was always a bright, sunny day in Squirm so this might have been just any ordinary day. Only it wasn't. In a town where happiness was a way of life, there was a controversy brewing that threatened the peace and harmony of the entire town of Squirm.

It all began with a small, dark cloud drifting overhead. A dark cloud this miniscule would go completely unnoticed anywhere else in the world, but not in Squirm. You see, dark clouds were not a common sight there -- in fact the majority of residents had only heard of them but had never seen one -- so when one made its appearance, it caused quite a stir amongst the citizens of Squirm, or Squirmonians as they were called. People gathered in awe, as if they were watching an eclipse, to stare at this floating phenomenon.

The children looked in complete wonderment at this "thing" they were seeing and asked their parents what it was. Their parents, however, being just as unfamiliar with this skyward thing, were at a loss to explain it. The most noticeable characteristic of this event was the Squirmonians' reactions.

While others might have become nervous and panicky in this situation, fearing impending doom, Squirmonians, true to their nature, became curious. Being the inquisitive lot they were, they wanted to know what brought this dark cloud their way, and sought to learn more about it.

Questions began to surface: What is it? Where did it come from? What does it mean? Is there anything inside of it? Why is it dark? Will it move? How big can one of these things get? Can it fall and hit us on the head? What makes it stay up there?

When answers were not forthcoming, the townspeople turned to their one dependable source of learning, Professor Squirm.

"Alas," answered Professor Sunny Squirm, the town's mayor, "this is what the world is really like out there beyond Squirm, and it appears to have reared its ugly head here today. It is the signal that the Squelchers are at work. We do not need to be afraid of them; we simply need to understand them, to learn about them, and to help them with their habit of squelching. You see, Squelchers are resistors -- they hate to learn and they hate to squirm. It's unbelievable but true."

A movement against Squirming was building steam, and the town was beginning to realize how vulnerable they were and how vulnerable their closely-held principles were to those who were afraid and threatened by them.

To understand Squirmonians one must understand the town's founder. Professor Sunny Squirm is credited with starting a tiny village, which ultimately became Squirm. He was a larger-than-life individual who embodied all of the traits that Squirmonians held so dear. His tolerance of others, his passion to learn, his way of encouraging others to learn, his patience as people were learning, and above all, his personal quest to continuously learn, made him the living example of all that Squirmonians aspired to be. Sunny was one of the most knowledgeable people alive, yet his humility about what he knew -- he never acted like a know-it-all -- kept his fertile mind in a constant state of curiosity that stimulated learning. Not only was he a constant learner, but he relished the opportunity to relearn so he could re-experience the original joy of discovery. In the process of relearning, he always learned something new. He considered learning to be a fountain of youth, *his* fountain of youth.

Sunny was a tall, slender, stately-looking man who always had a smile on his face. He was not young, but he had a youthful appearance and demeanor that never seemed to show his age. If youthful vigor was an attitude, he certainly had it. It pleased Squirmonians to cross his path during the day because his radiant smile had a magical effect on them. No one quite understood how or why it had such a powerful effect on them, but it did. And Sunny's brightness -- there was no other way to describe it -- always seemed to spread in all directions.

Sunny had his bad days, just like everyone else, but unlike most, he had the remarkable capacity not to let problems define his life or control his attitude. In fact bad days were also seen as good days, because, as Sunny would say, "Without bad days, how would you recognize the good ones?

There's a lesson to be learned in most things, if one only looks. Be a seeker; that's how you'll find it."

People just seemed to gravitate to Professor Squirm. He was the quintessential leader. People liked being in his presence, felt great when he was around, and were encouraged in each of their endeavors no matter how small or great. Gradually, individuals began taking on his characteristics, creating a growing and vibrant community. As their small village expanded, the people asked Professor Squirm to be its leader and he graciously accepted. And so it was that this unique and humble person formed the town of Squirm.

Learning -- continuous learning -- was the cornerstone upon which this new town was founded. What was so incredible about the Professor and the residents of this town was the way they always wanted to squirm because *squirming* meant you were *learning*. Countless lessons were there for the taking, and Squirmonians recorded the lessons they learned in a most unique fashion.

One of Professor Squirm's most delightful characteristics was his ability to think and talk in rhyme. Often, as he learned something new, he created a short poem that would help him remember his lesson. It was how he remembered things. Squirmonians loved Sunny's poetic tendencies and they decided they wanted all of their lessons in the form of a rhyme. Thus, Mayor Squirm created an official position on the Mayoral staff, The Rhythmic Squimatic, and his short little poems became known as Squimmericks. The original Squimmerick is on a piece of parchment which to this day adorns the main rotunda in the Town Hall. It serves as a constant reminder of the Town's guiding principle…the principle of Squirming.

Sunny helped people realize how much they could achieve if only they tried. He also helped them understand that a feeling of discomfort and even a little fear was very common to learning. He described this feeling as *squirming*. Squirming was not only a common feeling when you were learning something new, it was a necessary feeling if you were learning.

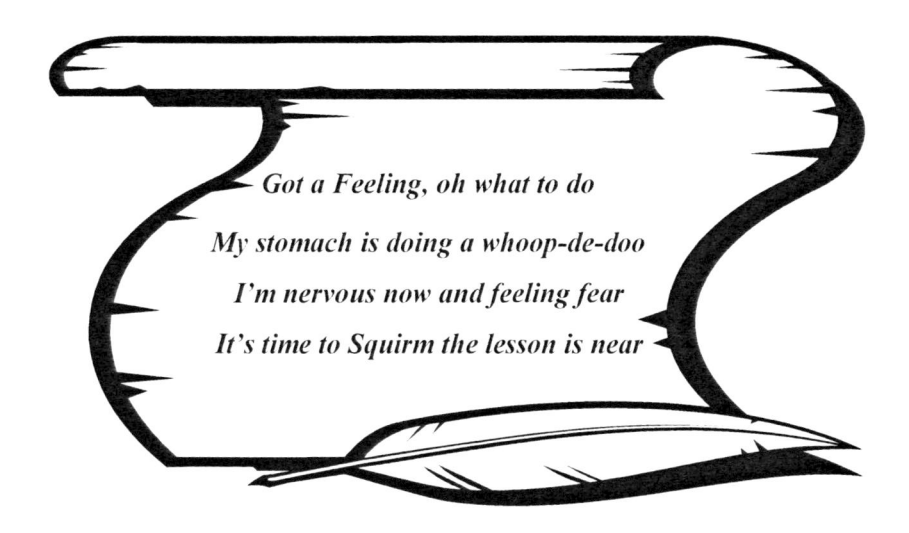

> *Got a Feeling, oh what to do*
> *My stomach is doing a whoop-de-doo*
> *I'm nervous now and feeling fear*
> *It's time to Squirm the lesson is near*

Sunny's dream of an entire community of Squirmers had come into being. So it was that when the dark cloud of doubt arrived on the scene, the Squirmonians reacted in their typical fashion -- they welcomed it. It was obvious to Sunny, and a handful of others, that a major Squirm was about to occur. Most Squirmonians were unaware that they were about to begin squirming like they never had before.

My altitude and latitude

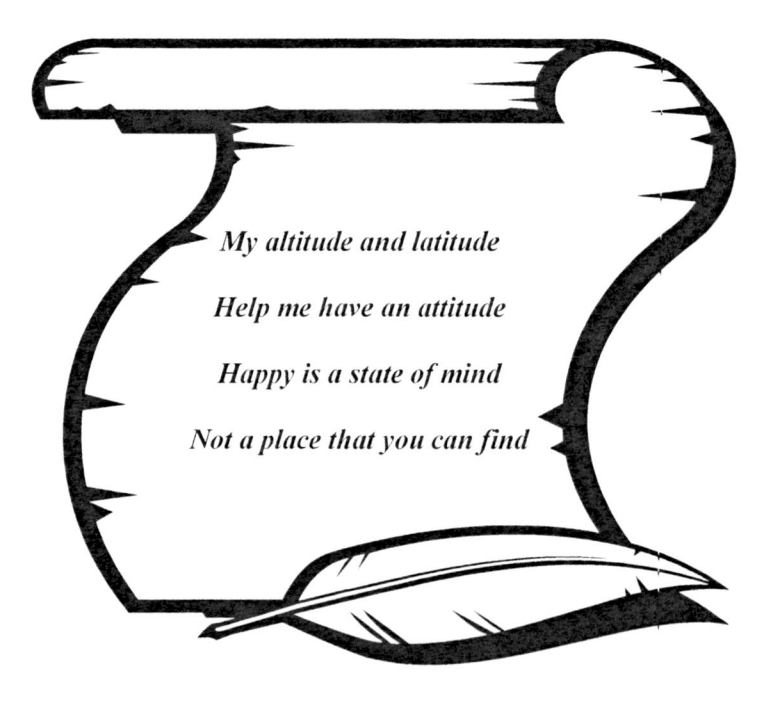

Help me have an attitude

Happy is a state of mind

Not a place that you can find

Chapter Three:
The Great Divide

New challenges were now facing the little town of Squirm. It all started when that gray cloud showed up. You see, Squirm was "The Learningest Place in the World." That's who had come there to live. That was what adults taught their offspring. All in all, learning was as important to Squirmonians as water, air, and food -- it was life-sustaining.

Unfortunately, even in this wonderful learning environment, there were certain people attempting to change the town's "high fallutin'" learning ways.

One would think that the growth, prosperity, and eternal optimism in Squirm would be more than anyone could wish for. However, there was a small faction in the town which was deeply threatened by all the learning that was occurring. In fact, Squirming was not only frowned upon by these learn-resisters, it was considered downright obscene.

At first, individual Squelchers hid their anti-learning ways. But as they found one another, they banded together and became more organized.

Once in a group, they stopped being an easily ignored underground movement and became a force great enough to be reckoned with. Slowly and methodically, they started undermining learning and life in the town of Squirm. The differences between the Squelchers and the Squirmonians were becoming more and more divisive.

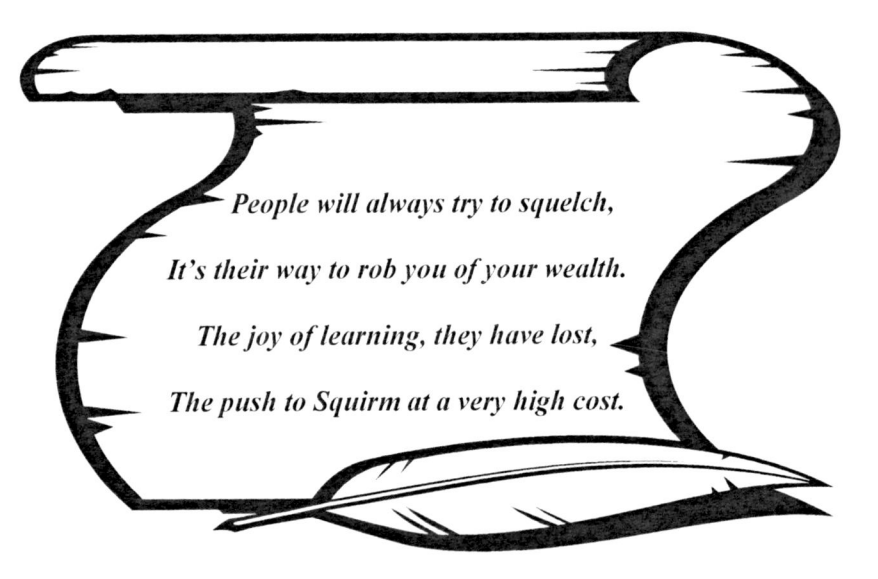

> *People will always try to squelch,*
>
> *It's their way to rob you of your wealth.*
>
> *The joy of learning, they have lost,*
>
> *The push to Squirm at a very high cost.*

Squirmonians had known all along there were Squelchers roaming the earth, but not in vast numbers and certainly not in herds. The new phenomenon Squirms were dealing with was perplexing to them because they had never had to deal with a threat on this scale before. Indeed, new times had arrived, and with them new opportunities to learn. Would Squirmonians rise the occasion? They always had before.

Mayor Squirm called a town hall meeting to help Squirmonians deal with the dark cloud of doubt that was holding firmly in place. In fact, one observant Squirmonian noticed it had grown slightly since its arrival less than a day ago. Why was it getting larger?

In another part of town, another group was meeting for what they considered to be an equally important reason. Their *gripe session* was the first formally organized Squelch Session ever recorded. Their dread of, distaste for, and outright repulsion of learning brought these birds of a feather together, and now their movement had a membership roster large enough to make noise…lots of noise.

Squelchers were a stubborn breed, and proud of it. They adopted a code of resistance to learning which held that anything new was bad, and anything old was good. Squelchers believed that learning new things would ultimately lead to change. **Change!** It was a bad word to use around Squelchers. And why did things always change? Because people just wouldn't stop their doggone, irritating habit of learning. So, Squelchers fought learning whenever they had the chance.

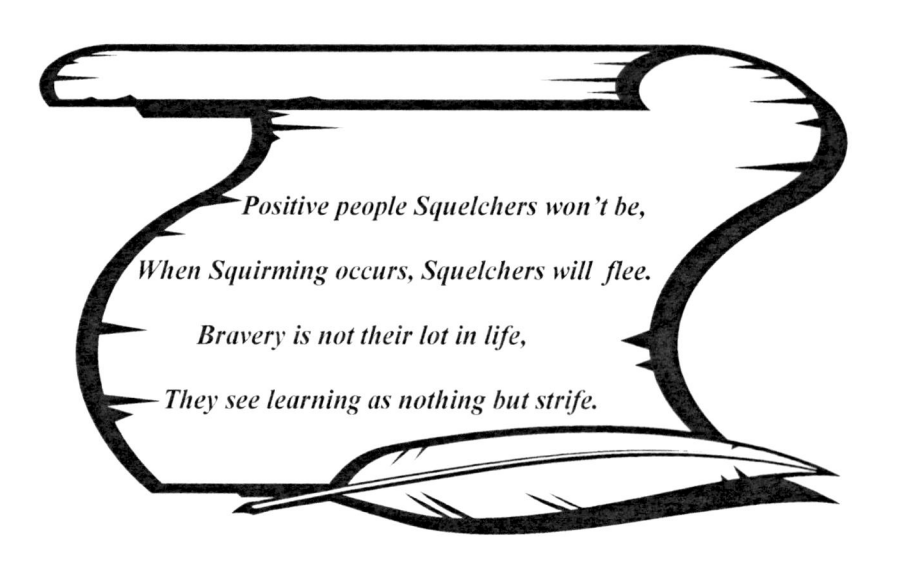

> *Positive people Squelchers won't be,*
> *When Squirming occurs, Squelchers will flee.*
> *Bravery is not their lot in life,*
> *They see learning as nothing but strife.*

Initially, squelching was nothing more than an easily ignored undercurrent of criticism and complaining, but as it gained favor it became a way of life. New Squelchers were enlisted into the small cadre of the passionately pessimistic poops[*]. As the number of Squelchers grew, the town of Squirm became crowded. Predictably, the town wasn't big enough for both of them. The overcrowding was making life difficult, and it was evident that one group had to go.

---

[*] Author's note. This is the first book of its type to call these people what they really are.

As the townspeople came together in an attempt to reconcile their differences, it became obvious that their divide was irreparable. Each side had vested interest in their beliefs and unwillingness to compromise. Squirmonians were a compassionate, understanding lot because they had learned how from all the Squirming they had each done. However, when it came to learning or not learning, nothing was negotiable. Squirming was a part of their life, their town, and their heritage. It must remain.

Squelchers wanted to eliminate learning, to put a cap on it, so to speak. They stubbornly believed that when you knew enough you didn't need to know more. All that knowledge was a form of greed, and greed was a form of gluttony, and wasn't gluttony, after all, one of the seven deadly sins? The Squelchers kept offering stupid arguments like this, which would have continued to this day if someone (a Squirmonian no doubt) had not pointed out the futility of the effort. The Squelchers argued that if Squirms liked to squirm so much, THEY should be the ones to leave. After all, that way they could really *Squirm*! THEY could build a new town where THEY could learn a new and better way while squirming in the process. (Squelchers were, and are, good at coming up with all sorts of irresponsible arguments they actually believe.) Squirmonians, who were always ready to tackle a new opportunity, slowly came to agree with the Squelchers.

In the end, it was decided that there would be two towns: one where Squirming was allowed and one where it was not. Hence the town of Squelch was born out of resistance, negativity, and pessimism.

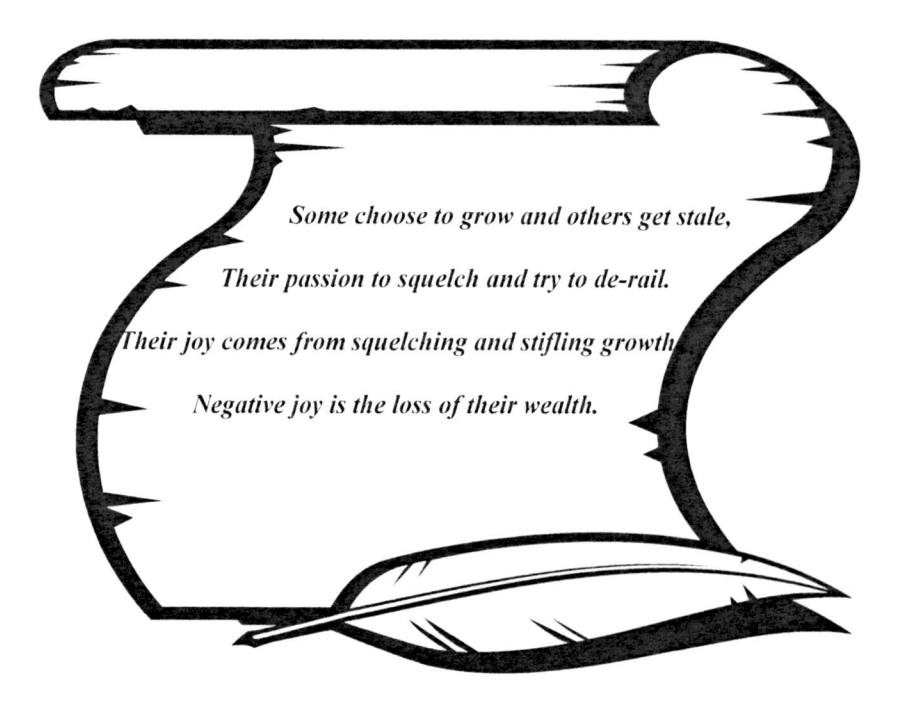

> *Some choose to grow and others get stale,*
>
> *Their passion to squelch and try to de-rail.*
>
> *Their joy comes from squelching and stifling growth*
>
> *Negative joy is the loss of their wealth.*

The Squelchers, who pretended to be courageous but were actually too frightened to leave, were to take over the town of Squirm, while the Squirmonians were to build a new place to live. Mayor Sunny Squirm said the new town of Squirm would be a "better place to learn and squirm." Moving was going to be a wonderful opportunity

to acquire new knowledge and to make new discoveries -- all the Squirmonians agreed.

The Squirmonians set their departure date, made arrangements, and found a new location for their town. The move was on.

As the last Squirmonian departed the beloved town of Squirm, now known as Squelch, the sun wasn't shining quite as brightly, and the usual feeling of optimism had turned into a sense of gloom. One could feel it in the air. Dark clouds of doubt were beginning to multiply.

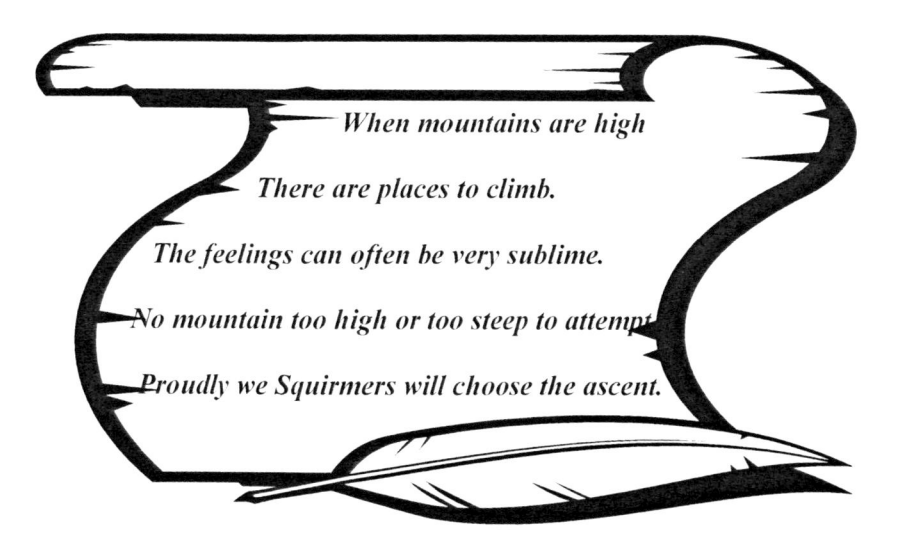

When mountains are high

There are places to climb.

The feelings can often be very sublime.

No mountain too high or too steep to attempt

Proudly we Squirmers will choose the ascent.

Chapter Four:
A Hidden Traitor

With the last Squirmonian gone, the town of Squelch was officially formed. Its residents became known as Squelchonians, and they immediately began dismantling the learning apparatus that the Squirmonians had so passionately constructed. Now they needed a leader. But whom would they choose?

All signs pointed to one individual, the originator of the Squelching movement and the most outspoken opponent of learning they could find, a certain Nils Stifle. Nils, a big-mouthed renegade, might have been considered an outlaw of sorts by many, but he was a true hero to the weak-minded few who believed in his cause and fell prey to his negativity.

Nils Stifle certainly was the antithesis of a Squirmonian. It was always puzzling, even now, how Stifle could have lived as long as he did in a town like Squirm. He could have found a great many supporters elsewhere, but he took special pleasure in the challenges that a town like Squirm had posed. Living there had required special talents and a great deal of effort. He managed to survive through his covert activities. He was obviously a good actor, going through the motions of being a learner, but deep down inside he resented, fought, and resisted learning with all his might.

Stifle was a natural born pessimist who developed the ability to find the negative in anything positive. Many wondered in awe how he did it, and his ability to gain enthusiastic supporters for his non-productive causes became legendary.

Colleagues who gravitated to Stifle's cause had not been in abundance in a town like Squirm, but there was one here, another there, who had the Squelching tendency and did not need much encouragement to let their resistance to learning surface. Through his unrelenting efforts of whining, complaining, and campaigning, he developed followers. When he had enough, he went public along with them. That's when the dark cloud of doubt showed up. Now it was obvious, Stifle was their guy. He would be the first mayor of Squelch.

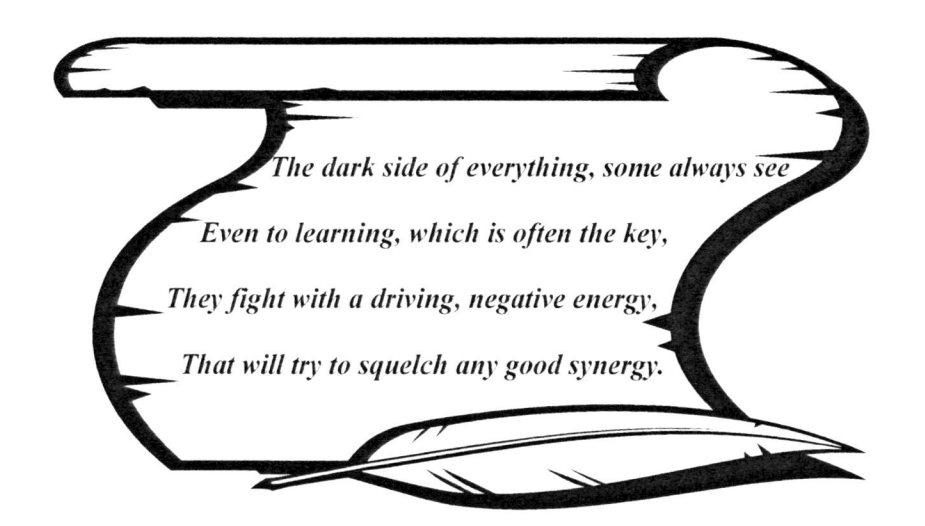

The dark side of everything, some always see
Even to learning, which is often the key,
They fight with a driving, negative energy,
That will try to squelch any good synergy.

During his inaugural address as Mayor, Stifle proudly proclaimed, "We've fought hard so we don't have to learn, and we won't. If individuals want to learn and grow and, forgive me for saying this word publicly, SQUIRM, they can go live somewhere else! They're not welcome here. This town was built on the infallible fault-line we call The Comfort Zone and that's where it will stay.

"Learning causes change and change is bad. Change threatens the destruction of The Comfort Zone we fought so hard to establish. As your Mayor, I promise to fight learning every day." Then Stifle's tone turned deadly serious, and the jubilation died down a bit. He addressed the crowd in a somber and determined way, "And to those who live among us who want to learn, we know who you are."

Stifle was referring to the Squinches in Squelch. Squinches were those who pretended to not be learners; they were counterfeit Squelchonians. Underneath, deep inside themselves, they had a fire burning, a desire to learn. They had to douse it frequently, but the urge to learn was always just beneath the surface. But fear of reprisal and loss of the approval of the significant others in their lives kept their learning to a minimum, though it never completely stopped it. Since they were underground, they certainly couldn't share any of their newfound knowledge with Squelchonians lest they be discovered. So discreetly they lived their lives, learning and denying it.

Stifle continued. "I say this, and Squinches and Squirmers, you had better listen: We don't need any of you rebellious types here. We'll find you and root you out. And Squinches, don't think you can go unnoticed for very long. We know when people are learning because it shows in their attitude. You may think you're good actors, but you can't be that good. However, we know how desperately you desire to stop learning and to break the habit, so what I offer you today is amnesty. If any Squinch voluntarily turns him or herself in, we will offer you free counseling to end that senseless desire you have toward learning. It will all be absolutely free for as long as it takes to kill the desire inside you to learn. Fear not. The end of learning is near."

At this, the citizenry became tumultuous, as cheers and whistles and applause drowned out the Mayor's speech.

Amidst all the cheers and hoopla from the townspeople, there was one in the crowd whose reactions to the message were quite subdued. Wanta Wiggle was now an official Squelchonian. But she had a dark secret -- she was actually a Squinch. Indeed, Wanta had fallen in love with a Squelcher though she was unaware of it at the time, and she married him, believing she had found the Squirmer of her dreams. Shortly after their wedding, though, Wanta realized that Stew was anything but a Squirmer. She had married a died-in-the-wool Squelcher. Oddly enough, she still loved him and felt over time, she could help his learning abilities to resurface. She knew he had Squirming potential and she vowed to help him as much as she could (without his knowing).

Stew, for his part, had begun the work of Squelching within his home; and by the time the Squirmonians had left, with Wanta not going with them, he believed he had successfully made a Squelcher of her. Little did he know that instead of a Squelcher, he had turned her into a Squinch.

Wanta was forced to keep her true Squirming nature a well-guarded secret that she shared with no one. She found herself in a huge predicament. Wanting to do the right thing, because she was a woman of character, she stuck by Stew and held her Squirming nature at bay. She also believed that she would be able to change Stew's Squelching behavior in due course.

When she and her family (which also consisted of two children, twin boys named Willy and Wally) lived in Squirm, she was able to find relief with others like herself -- people stuck in a non-learning environment -- and quench her thirst for knowledge and learning by keeping company with them. Her home life was acceptable then, but now, without the kinship and support of her Squirmacious allies, she had to learn a whole new way of life.

As she pondered her situation, she mused that she now had the same but opposite role that Nils Stifle had had in Squirm. While Stifle had been a Squelching Squirmer, Wanta was instead a Squirming Squelcher. Odd. However, she knew, being the true learner that she was, she would find a way to be happy. After all, becoming a Squinch was just another chance to learn, and learn she would. And yes, she decided, as the Mayor rambled on and on and on, that she would not turn herself in. *Who knows?* she said to herself. *Maybe some day they'll need a Squinch in this town. If that day ever comes, I'll be ready.*

As Mayor Stifle ended his blustery, boring inaugural address, the clouds continued multiplying in number. The initial dark cloud of doubt had become two, then four, then eight. Now the sky had darkened and dark clouds of doubt were everywhere. In Squelch, there just didn't seem to be much on the horizon.

Chapter Five:
The Excuse Factory

Wanta Wiggle stayed underground. She was a Squirmer and she knew it. She tried to not learn, but no amount of effort on her part could stifle that hunger. She ultimately came to accept her love of learning but decided that she would not allow her thirst for knowledge to be seen by anyone, her family included. Above all, she feared the happiness-deprivation interventions, which Squelch was famous for, and so she zealously protected her deepest desires. She always felt that she was living two lives, and that no one really knew her. This was of course true. She had developed the ability to act and talk like a Squelch, but deep in her heart she was a Squirmer waiting to sprout wings.

Wanta kept her learning a deep, dark secret. Recognized as a pillar of the Squelchonian community, she was promoted to a position of importance at the company where she worked. The Whinery, noticing her brilliance, had chosen her to serve in a leadership capacity, fast-tracking her career to the top. She served as the CEO of The Excuse Factory, the most productive and profitable division of The Whinery. As the Chief

Excuse Officer, she headed a team of Squelchers who were responsible for creating some of the most famous excuses ever contrived.

Many people found these excuses utterly enticing and completely irresistible and bought them readily. What was most interesting was how one excuse begot another excuse. They seemed to spontaneously generate. Entire lines of excuses, targeted at specific situations, were a testimony to the brilliance of The Excuse Makers at The Excuse Factory.

Wanta was often concerned that her adeptness at creating new excuses was a demonstration of her depth of knowledge and feared that a Squelch might notice it. But as long as the negative excuses kept coming, they deterred a closer look at her brilliance. She also adopted a strategy of developing some lame excuses. This kept most Squelches convinced that she was one of them. Some of her "lame" excuses were very shoddy, but when she received criticism for them, she casually reminded the criticizer of the company's motto: A bad excuse is better than no excuse at all.

For years, The Excuse Factory division of The Whinery had produced legendary excuses. They had a broad, worldwide market and had trouble keeping up with the demands. Overtime and long hours at work were not uncommon in the early years, but lately things had slowed down.

Unbeknownst to most of the Squelchonians, the market for excuses was drying up. Wanta had taken note of this, and began wondering how the town of Squelch could survive if it lost its main industry. She knew that she could not address the problem because that would show initiative, raising suspicions of her Squirmacious nature. So she continued to manufacture excuses, reserved exclusively for The Excuse Factory, as to why things were not going as they should.

Deep in the recesses of her mind, she secretly hoped there would come a day when she could squirm out loud. So she waited.

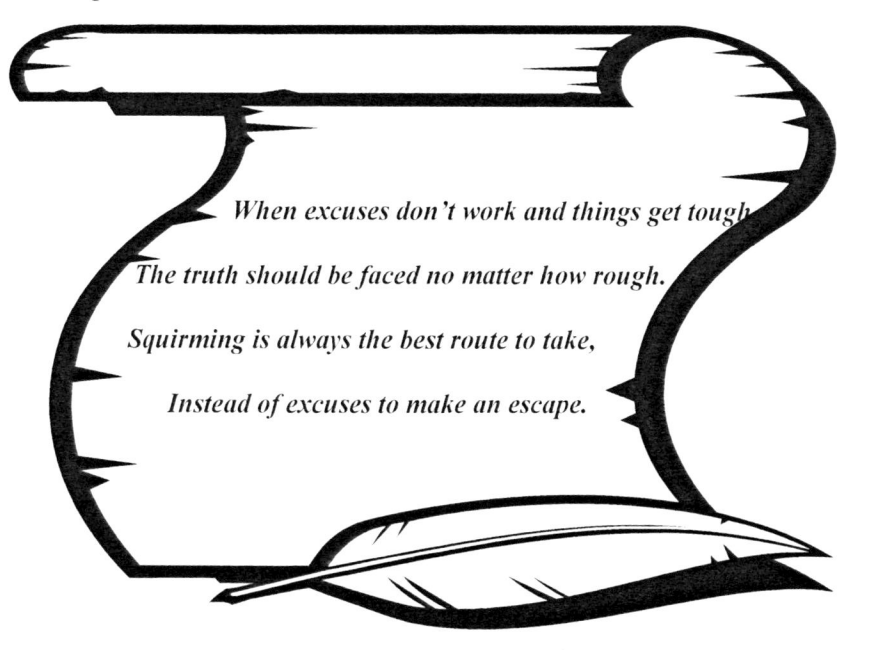

When excuses don't work and things get tough,

The truth should be faced no matter how rough.

Squirming is always the best route to take,

Instead of excuses to make an escape.

Chapter Six:
The Town of Squelch

Years passed in the town of Squelch, and very little changed. Nothing there was new. Indeed, anything new was frowned upon and met with stiff resistance. While Squelchonians were perfectly contented, (or at least professed to be) they were clearly living in a rut. Stagnancy was the only word that adequately described their way of life.

A walk down the main street in town, Ambivalent Avenue, clearly demonstrated the mundane lives that these people had chosen.

The most popular restaurant in Squelch was Larry Leftover's Diner. Larry had legally changed his last name to Leftover, and was known as Lefty. Someone (obviously a Squirmonian) once pointed out that Lefty was right-handed, so he became nicknamed Right-Handed Lefty -- an unusual name, but no one in Squelch had ever noticed the contradiction.

Right-handed Lefty's daily fare included the best of yesterday. Since no one ever ordered fresh food, Right-handed Lefty always cooked tomorrow's food today. This served one of the

Squelcher's most basic physiological needs, eating food from the good old days, or in this case, the good old day.

"Hey Right-handed Lefty," many a Squelchonian would ask, "What's today's special?"

"Leftover Tuna Noodle Casserole," he would reply.

"Wow, that's great," they'd say. "I'll have that. Give me a double portion."

The daily special at Larry Leftover's Diner had been leftover tuna noodle casserole since the day the diner had opened some eighteen years earlier, although to say that it had NEVER changed would be a slight inaccuracy.

Right-handed Lefty, considering himself a chef in the order of the great French master chefs, decided one day to surprise the unsuspecting townspeople and changed the daily special. He offered them a sumptuous concoction of leftover macaroni and cheese, dried out just the way it should be, all clumped together and congealed. Sure it was delicious, but when several of the usual patrons asked what the daily special was, they were shocked and dismayed to hear "leftover macaroni and cheese" pour forth from the lips of the town's most popular restaurateur. It caused a major ruckus.

Many Squelchonians gathered together, formed a picket line outside of the diner, and protested the change. A week-long boycott of Larry Leftover's Diner soon taught Right-handed Lefty a valuable lesson about life in Squelch: Don't Change Things. That was twelve years ago, and nothing had changed since.

While many of the town's old-timers still fondly recalled their efforts at stifling the menu change, proudly claiming the current menu as a testimony to their triumphant victory, Squirmers who got wind of the story marveled at how so much human energy could be wasted on such an insignificant matter. One Squirmonian, a writer for a popular magazine, picked up on the story and wrote a series of essays titled "The Tuna Noodle Casserole Chronicles." He received acclaim for his exposé of the event, and even won a major publishing award for it.

An automobile dealership which opened the same month the town of Squelch formed, was located on the corner of Ambivalent Avenue and Lackluster Lane. Here, relics of the past were proudly displayed as the best cars in town. Tried, tested, and well broken-in, the wares at Charley's Uzed

Carz were said to be "the best transportation money can buy." Charley frequently reminded car shoppers that new-fangled cars just didn't measure up to the cars he sold. His had stood the test of time. Since most Squelchonians didn't like change and preferred to keep what they had, there wasn't a brisk market for cars in Squelch. There was that rare occasion, however, when a "new" old car seemed necessary, as in the case of a family that had grown. Off to Charley's they would go to find the best new old car that they could find. Oddly enough, the cars on Charley's lot just seemed to keep recycling.

There had been only one new one in the past ten years, as a result of some visitor in town abandoning his vehicle. The car had broken down on a visit to Squelch so he hung around waiting for it to be repaired. Unfortunately, no one knew how to fix a new car. No one bothered to tell the visitor that. However, after three days in Squelch, he said he began to feel like he was going insane due to all of the negativity. He was a happy person and smiled a lot but that caused problems because people thought he was sick. He left town in a hurry leaving his vehicle and all of his belongings behind. No one ever heard from him again.

A large sign hung over Charley's Uzed Carz lot which read,

> *Old is new and new is bad,*
>
> *Charley's Carz will make you glad.*
>
> *Our cars are tested, tried and true,*
>
> *Don't come here for something new.*

On the street behind Charley's car lot was the town's main clothing and apparel store. Harriet's Hand-Me-Down-Clothing Nook proudly occupied half of the block on Stifle Street. A massive knotty pine showroom housed Nehru jackets, bell-bottoms, silk shirts and other clothing of all manner and description. Clothing from bygone days proudly hung on the racks, over which a continuous stream of eager shoppers and fashion aficionados salivated. Harriet believed that these pre-worn garments would help any Squelchonian make the appropriate fashion statement.

"Clothes make the person," Harriet often said, "and when you want to show your proud Squelching ways, your clothes help you make a statement." Harriet gathered clothes from the dust piles of the world, looking for the shabbiest pre-worn clothing she could find.

Many a Squelchonian would brag about who had worn his or her clothing in its previous life, boldly proclaiming that "If it was good enough for them, it's more than good enough for me."

It had often been thought that the newest fashion trends that brought back old styles started in Squelch, but it wasn't true. Threadbare garments never caught on anywhere except in Squelch.

One of the major annual events in Squelch was Harriet's Annual Garment Grab Bag. Traffic was clogged during the one-day sale. Brown paper bags, stuffed with an unimaginable array of clothing and sealed tightly, kept one from knowing what they were buying. But since the clothing was pre-worn and cheap, it was a low-risk investment for the average Squelchonian.

The town of Squelch was similar to Squirm in one way -- there was no place else in the world like it. However, the similarities ended there. Visitors of Squelch, mostly curiosity seekers, were few and far between. They fell into one of two categories. The vast majority of visitors couldn't wait to leave. The remaining ones found a place where they felt right at home. They were, of course, latent Squelchers who had never before experienced the pure, unbridled joylessness of negativity and pessimism that greeted them in Squelch. Many chose to stay. They quickly assimilated into the community and began living the joyless life about which they had so eagerly dreamed.

There was only one problem for these new Squelchonians – their children. Many of their children possessed curiosity and the desire to learn far beyond their need to do so. This confused and befuddled most Squelchers, who found curiosity to be an annoying trait worthy of punishment. So, leaders of the community formed a task force charged with the responsibility of stifling all Squirming urges. They even put together a team of scientists who were convinced that there was a learning gene, an inherited trait, and that the desire for learning ran in certain families. They were trying to discover a way to "cleanse" people who had the problem gene, although it was hard to do this without learning anything new.

The generally accepted rule in Squelch was that children should learn slowly and then stop when they had learned "quite enough." Most Squelchonian children were accepting of these instructions from their elders, who obviously knew what was best, but the new Squelcher children were not as eager to agree. These "fast learners," as they were called, required special de-education classes. And since children tend to be eager learners, it often took years of brainwashing to squelch and stifle their desires. Squelchonian children's quest to learn could typically be completely squelched and stifled by their late teen years. Truly gifted Squelcher students quit learning much earlier in life.

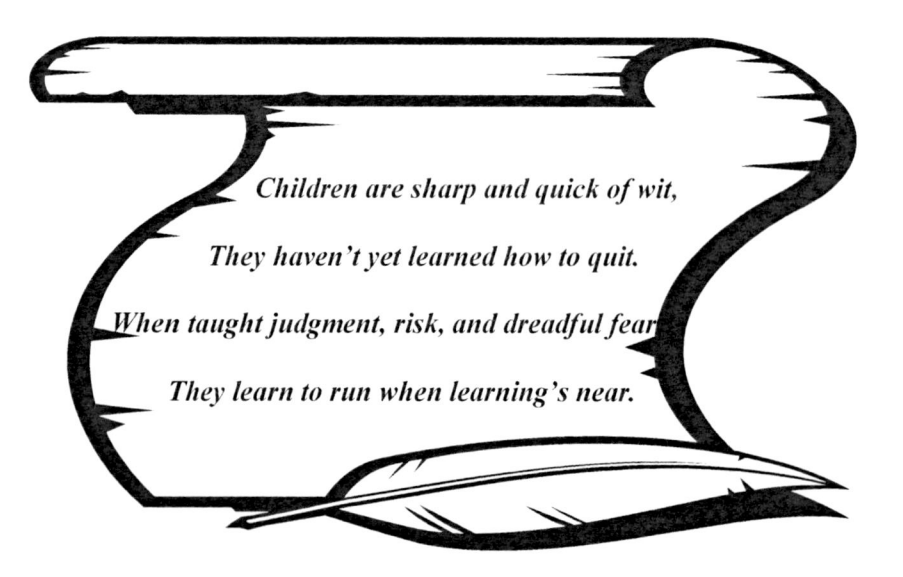

Children are sharp and quick of wit,

They haven't yet learned how to quit.

When taught judgment, risk, and dreadful fear

They learn to run when learning's near.

Sometimes, though, during their rebellious teenage years, young people began showing signs of Squirmability. This trait had to be dealt with quickly in a firm and efficient way. Every Squelchonian knew that Squirmability, left unchecked, could undermine and threaten the very fabric of Squelch society.

Basic level Squelch and Stifle classes usually cured the problem. In some of the more difficult cases, huge doses of negativity, pessimism, coupled with round-the-clock whining by some of the greatest whiners in the world, ultimately solved the conundrum. Sometimes, Advanced Excuse-making Classes were also prescribed as an antidote to Squirmability. Usually after several weeks of happiness deprivation, along with exposure to the mainstream media and the archived tapes of Nils Stifle, the most positive attitude could be turned around. Indeed, the town prided itself on the fact that they had successfully eliminated the thirst for learning in every person they had encountered since the formation of the town of Squelch.

You can't, you won't, it's not possible,
Your dreamed-up talent isn't plausible.
If you believe that you will surely see,
You'll never become what you really could be.

Chapter Seven:
The Family That Complains Together, Remains Together

Like his wife Wanta, Stew was a prominent citizen of Squelch. The Wiggles lived in their split-level home on Whining Way with their two boys, Willy and Wally. Not only was Stew a devoted family man and husband, he was also a dedicated employee of the N& S Railroad where he occupied the exalted position of derailer. He was the best they had, and derailed more expertly and efficiently than anyone before him.

Stew had been a derailer most of his adult life. A solid upbringing at the hands of Squelcher parents brought out what they called was "the best of his abilities." He had not been an easy child – on many occasions he showed a passion to learn beyond what he needed to learn. His parents realized they were in for a rocky ride when Stew got an "A" on his report card. Frustrated and disappointed, his parents enrolled Stew in a Squelch and Stifle Intervention Program which finally, by his 17th birthday, turned Stew into a Squelcher. He was bright, there was no disputing that, and because he was so quick to learn, had become a very proficient negativist. (This obvious contradiction was never noticed.)

With his de-education complete, Stew joined the N & S railroad. No one knew what N & S stood for exactly. The original owners and founders of the railroad had heard that all railroads have initials, so theirs would too. They never worried much about what the N & S stood for; they were just initials and initials were a good thing when it came to railroads. But one day, an eavesdropping Stew Wiggle overheard the partners secretly admit that N & S stood for Negativity and Skepticism. "My kind of company," Stew said to himself.

Stew loved his work because he was so good at it. "When you do what you love, it's not work," he always said. His ability to derail, to get things off track, made him a local hero and the railroad the major industry of Squelch. No one had ever managed to get things as far off track as Stew, which guaranteed him a long career at N & S. Derailing was such an important part of the N & S culture, and Stew was the best at it.

The Whinery relied on the N & S for getting its excuses to market. Stew and his team were always on top of what needed to be done, and with their expertise, helped The Excuse Factory at The

Whinery become the leading excuse provider in the world.

Because they were involved in the two primary industries in Squelch, Stew and Wanta were pillars of their community. They were held up as the ideal couple, thought to have "a dream life," called "Mr. and Mrs. Normal" and "negativity at its best." When Squelchers looked at the Wiggles admiringly, they always said, "The family that complains together remains together."

From the outside looking in, theirs was the life every Squelchonian dreamed of living. But things were not as perfect as they seemed. Stew had the feeling, deep down inside himself, that Wanta was not a true Squelcher. He had never said anything to her about it; he hoped that he was wrong; but secretly he feared that Wanta was a Squinch, and he was terrified of anyone in Squelch finding out. Stew decided to address the problem when -- if -- the time came.

Wanta believed that her secret was completely safe. She had some similar concerns about Stew, though. Her intuition told her that Stew was a potential Squirmer. She believed that his de-education had suppressed, not destroyed, his desire to learn. She also felt that given the right opportunity, Stew's Squirminess might begin to surface again. *Perhaps,* she thought, *that's why I was so attracted to him. He's a Squirmer, underneath it all, I just know it. Someday, the worst of him will become the best of him.*

The best of us we cannot hide,

There's something in us deep inside.

The best comes out in time you see,

It can't be stopped, we all agree.

One night at their dinner table, the Wiggles said grace, thanking their creator for what they didn't know, and then promptly began feasting on a delicious meal of half-baked leftover spaghetti. It seemed like a normal night, until they began discussing a strange phenomenon spotted that afternoon.

"When did you see it?" Stew asked Wanta.

"I saw it at lunchtime," Wanta said. "How about you?"

"I was interrupted in a meeting and we all dashed outside to see it. I wonder what it means," Stew said.

Wanta thought she knew, but figured it would be best if she kept it to herself at this point. "I don't know. What do you think it means?" Since thinking wasn't encouraged in Squelch, she didn't expect much of a reply.

"I don't know," Stew answered, "but I think we had better figure it out."

This surprised Wanta. They were discussing one of those defining events, one of those happenings that change the course of lives and of history. Such an event had happened that day in Squelch, just like it had in Squirm many, many years earlier. Things were about to change.

Change is a constant that can't be changed

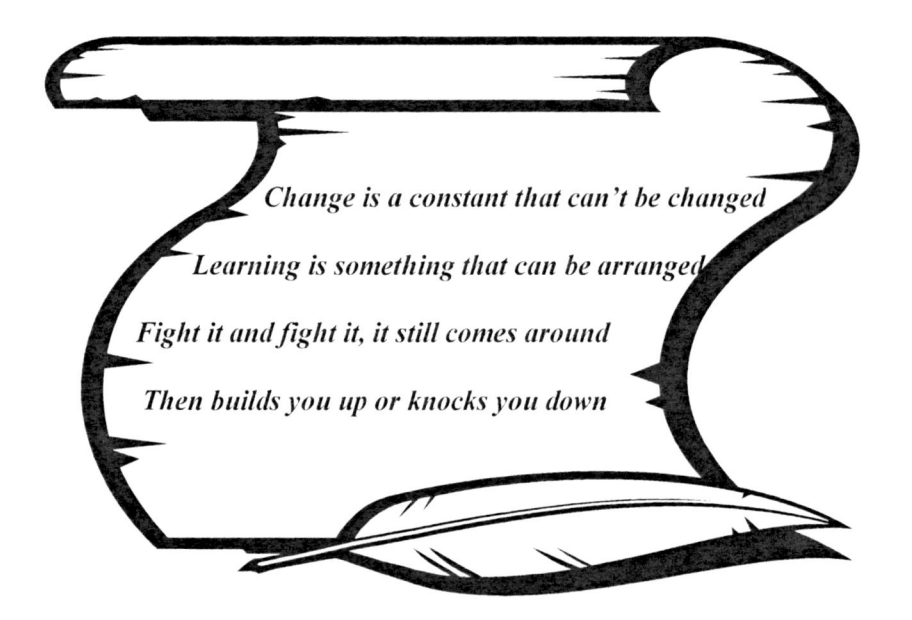

Learning is something that can be arranged

Fight it and fight it, it still comes around

Then builds you up or knocks you down

Chapter Eight:
A Strange Phenomenon

Earlier in the day, Stew was interrupted during a staff gripe session, one of the better ones they had had in quite some time. Negativity permeated the atmosphere and things were being expertly derailed when the meeting room door flung open.

"Come outside, Mr. Wiggle!" a frantic N & S railroad worker shouted at Stew. "It's amazing. You've got to see it!"

"See what?" Stew responded impatiently.

"I don't know what it is; I can't describe it. You just have to see it for yourself." With that, the worker hastily slammed the door and dashed back outside to stare in wonderment at the phenomenon.

Concerned, Stew quickly went outside to the freight yard to see what the commotion was all about. To his surprise, almost all of the N & S employees had gathered to witness the strange appearance in the sky. Spectators crowded the train yard and stood gazing heavenward, not understanding what they were witnessing. Some viewed it with wonderment, others with fear, and still others with calloused indifference. None knew what it was.

Since the formation of Squelch, dark clouds of doubt crowded the sky constantly. Doom and gloom in every direction were all Squelchonians ever saw. Today, however, there was a break in the clouds. It wasn't a big break, mind you, barely perceptible, but it was there. An observant Squelchonian (one of the few) had noticed a small ray of sun shining brightly through the dark clouds of doubt. While none of them knew what it was, many suspected that it had a greater significance than they could comprehend. How right they were.

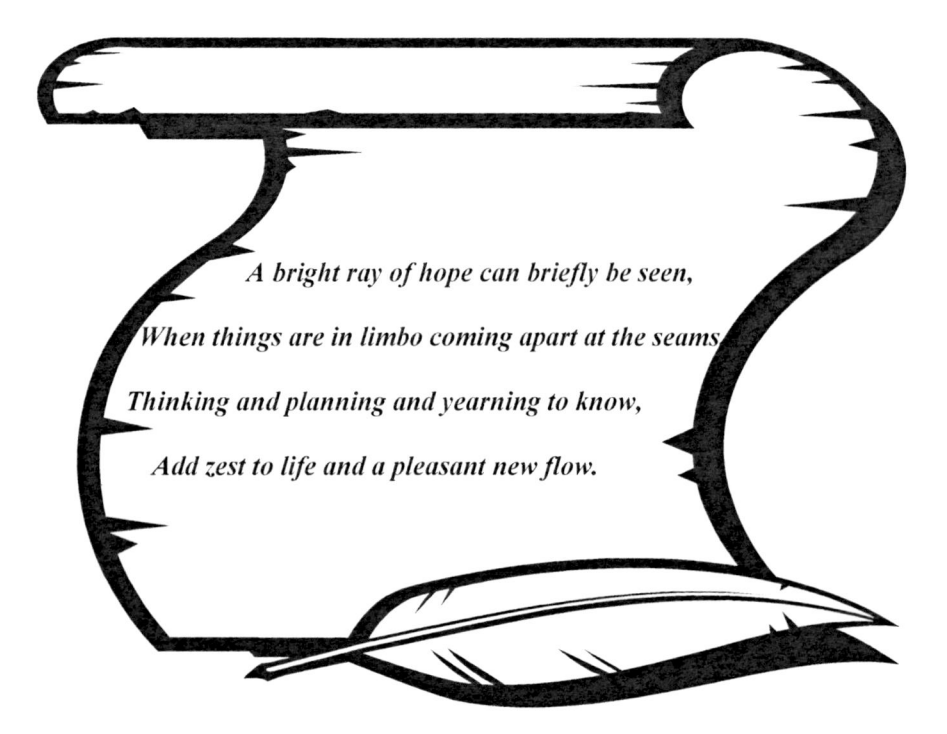

A bright ray of hope can briefly be seen,

When things are in limbo coming apart at the seams,

Thinking and planning and yearning to know,

Add zest to life and a pleasant new flow.

Chapter Nine
A Paradoxical Conundrum

Following dinner, Stew and Wanta, each still trying to figure out what the phenomenon meant, moved to the living room. After several minutes of silence, Wanta decided to take a risk. She blurted out, "I think trouble is on the horizon! I think we're in for a lot of turmoil, maybe even a big CHANGE!" There, she had said it. Let the chips fall where they may.

Stew, who had been slouching in his easy-chair, bolted upright at these words. "What do you mean?" he asked.

"I think something is happening that we don't understand," Wanta said. "That hole in the clouds means that something is different, something has happened or is happening, and we haven't figured out what it is, but we better." Stew was listening intently. Wanta continued, "I've noticed over the past couple of years that the need for new excuses has seemed to diminish. We've been stressed to the max trying to come up with new ones, and I cannot tell you how difficult that has been. It seems like everyone is using the same old excuses and that means that the demand for new ones has gone down. We've tried to invent new ones, irresistible excuses, but we haven't been able to find any. I'm very concerned. Haven't you noticed the slowdown at the N & S railroad?"

Stew thought for a moment, something that took a bit of effort on his part since he didn't do it that often, then replied, "Yes, now that you mention it, I think things have slowed down. I guess we just never paid much attention to it."

"We can't use the same old excuses, and we can't find any new ones that are worth anything. We've got a real problem here in Squelch, and I'm afraid if we don't address it we could be facing tough times ahead." Wanta was apprehensive to broach this topic, but if ever there was a time, this was it. The small ray of hope had caused many Squelchonians to take note. Wanta knew that if these people wanted to keep things the way they were, they would have to change. She almost chuckled at the thought.

Wanta continued, "I don't want to overreact here, but I also think that that break in the clouds was a signal that we had better wake up. I believe our town is threatened because the world has changed and we have not. Unless we begin addressing this, we are in for some serious tough times. Stew, I need you to be thinking about this and what we might do to get things back on track."

Thinking. Had he heard right? "But I'm a derailer. I don't know how to get things back on track. I've never had to." Stew was concerned, but he knew Wanta was dead right. He also knew that broaching this subject with the townspeople would be one of the toughest tasks either of them had faced in their lives.

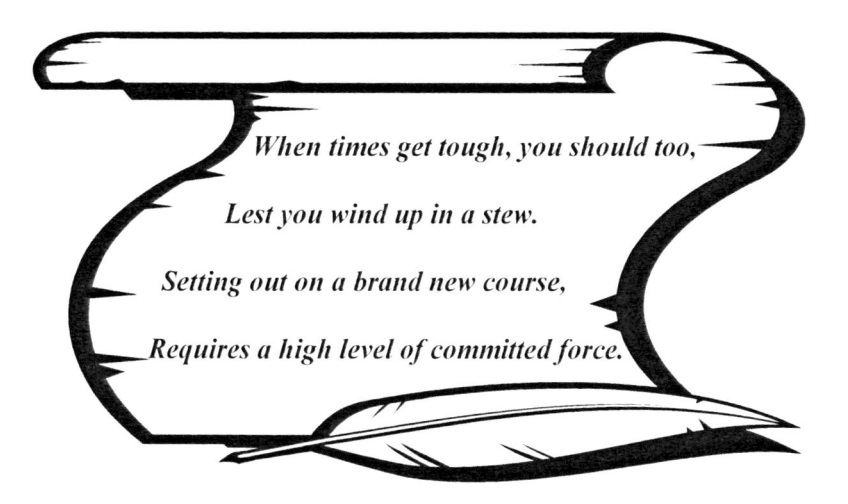

> *When times get tough, you should too,*
>
> *Lest you wind up in a stew.*
>
> *Setting out on a brand new course,*
>
> *Requires a high level of committed force.*

Wanta was feeling a level of invigoration that she had not experienced in years. She felt alive, younger. Stew, on the other hand, had done more thinking in one evening than he had done in the past several years. He was exhausted, though he did notice that he felt slightly less threatened, a bit less fearful than he had earlier in the day. He also felt a little less negative, and he was enjoying these foreign feelings. He wondered how he would feel about derailing tomorrow, given this new mindset he was starting to experience. But all this thinking had worn him out.

"I'm very tired," he said to Wanta. "I think I'm going to go to bed."

"You look tired," she said. "I'll join you shortly. I think I'm going to stay up a little longer and think about today and what it all means. Maybe I'll come up with something. We need some answers."

Stew retired and fell asleep almost immediately. That night he had some very unusual dreams, dreams that would change the course of history for the towns of Squelch and Squirm.

Chapter Ten:
Why The Whinery Wasn't Working

"I have an idea," Stew said to Wanta the following morning. The look of shock on her face was priceless. An idea from Stew was not what she expected. "Last night," he said, "I had a dream. I can't remember much of it, but what I do remember is that Squelch was in trouble. There was a lot of suffering and a lot of unhappiness because things had gotten so bad. Economic hard times made life almost unlivable, and people were being devastated by its impact. We were affected too. The N & S shut down because of a lack of work, and The Excuse Factory was nearing the same fate. A lot of people were returning their excuses to the factory, demanding a refund. The excuses weren't working, and the money-back guarantee The Excuse Factory offered was almost forcing it into bankruptcy. The Whinery was keeping The Excuse Factory afloat, but it couldn't do so forever. Even the whining was not working like had before. It was awful!"

Stew had Wanta's rapt attention, and she encouraged him to keep going. "The Whinery still had a market for its product -- complaining -- but all the complaining didn't fix the problem," he said. "Excuses were the real profit center of the enterprise, and without them the Whinery would eventually also face financial ruin. The more that Whinery people whined, the worse things got, and the more they whined. It was a vicious downward spiral. But guess what I saw? A ray of sunshine. Those dark clouds broke and a ray of sunshine appeared and suddenly, attitudes began changing. The town slowly began a comeback."

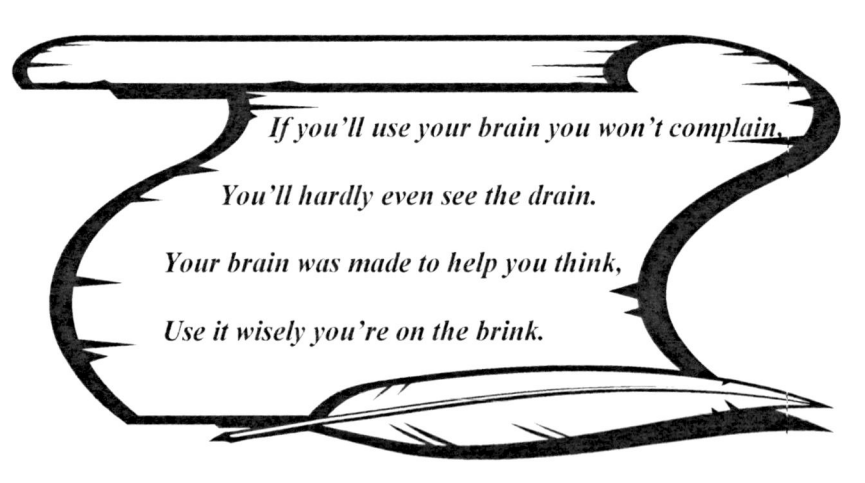

> *If you'll use your brain you won't complain,*
>
> *You'll hardly even see the drain.*
>
> *Your brain was made to help you think,*
>
> *Use it wisely you're on the brink.*

"What changed?" Wanta wanted to know.

"Attitudes -- pure and simple. What was even more amazing was that as the attitudes continued to change, there were less clouds and a bigger ray of sunshine." Stew reflected a bit more, then said, "All of a sudden I was a teenager again, and I began arguing and fighting with my negative teachers and other learning suppressors. It actually felt really good, and I dreamed that none of their anti-learning tactics took. I dreamed that instead of a derailer, I became a *re-railer*, and I liked it. I'm not sure where all of this is headed, but I feel different today. Somehow, I think you and I can help this town avert calamity, but only if we take the right approach."

"I totally agree," Wanta said. She was still a bit stunned from the radical change in Stew. "After you went to bed last night, I spent some time thinking. I basically came to the same conclusion. The arrival of that ray of sunshine is a great blessing. Squelch has been showing signs of trouble for quite a while, but they have mostly been ignored. Now, things are different. We have a reason to broach the subject with our friends, neighbors, and employees. It won't be easy because we have been a very change and learning-resistant people, but I know it is the right thing for us to do, and we must do it. Are you sure you're up for it?"

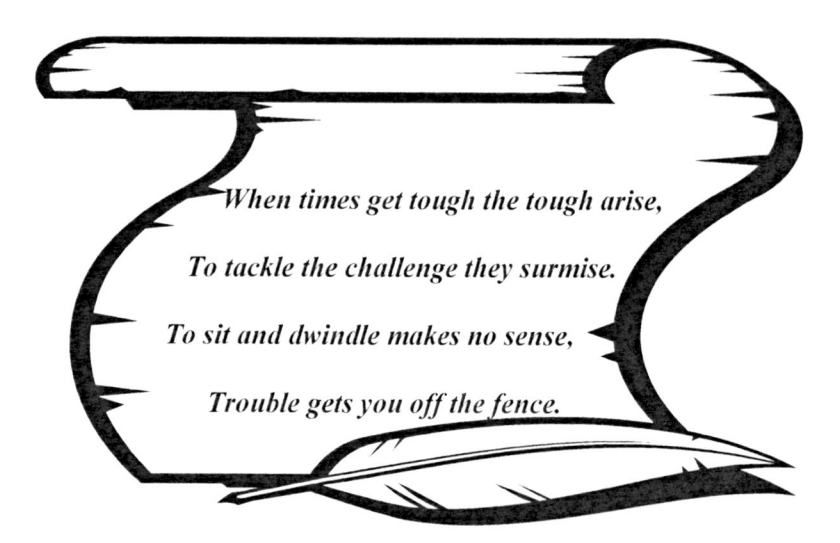

> *When times get tough the tough arise,*
>
> *To tackle the challenge they surmise.*
>
> *To sit and dwindle makes no sense,*
>
> *Trouble gets you off the fence.*

"Yes, I am," replied Stew. "I don't think we have a choice. My dream, which seemed too real to be just a dream, taught me something about myself. I may be more of a Squirmer than I ever thought I was. I realize now that I was always too worried about not fitting in, about what others would think. I guess that's the common thread that held all of us Squelchers together -- common negativity. Now, my worrying about rejection could cost our town dearly. It's time to save this town from itself and its rigid thinking, or should I say, non-thinking. But where do we start?"

This was the day that Wanta had lived for, the one she believed would inevitably come. She was ready. "I think there are certain people in Squelch who have shown they are not completely Squelchers."

"Who?" Stew wanted to know.

"Well, take Right-handed Lefty, for starters. Remember when he changed the menu that time? That's an indication to me of a person who could be approached. And how about Harriet? Remember that time she brought in all of those new clothes? That was risky and it showed at least a glimmer of changeability. And Charley Carz -- he had that new car on the lot for almost five years. He wanted to try something new, something different. He's a possibility as well. All of these people were willing to take a chance on something new and different. They'd be a good place to start."

"I think you are right. Do you think we should get together with them informally, build an alliance base and present the situation as we see it?"

"I think that sounds like a good idea." As she said it, Wanta noticed that for the first time in many, many years, she had used the word *think* a number of times in the same day and was not feeling guilty or worried about it. Her time might be drawing near; she might not have to be a Squinch forever. Maybe she could even Squirm again, and free herself from the bonds of negativity. Hope sprang inside her; she reveled in the idea of once again being a Squirmer instead of a Squinch.

But Stew and Wanta had to act fast, while the time was right, lest they miss their golden opportunity.

Chapter Eleven:
The Secret Meeting

Charley Carz, Harriet Houndstooth, and Right Handed Lefty sat motionless as Wanta and Stew explained the meaning of the small ray of hope everyone had witnessed. They had invited this small cadre of individuals to their home, explaining to each why they had been chosen for this get-together. Everyone had agreed to the total secrecy of what they were about to discuss. Stew and Wanta explained how they were apprehensive at even having a meeting like this, but that it was necessity. Before beginning, they also made it clear the topic might make some of them uncomfortable because it had to do with…Wanta hesitantly said the words she had not said to a stranger in years…"**Resistance to Learning and that creates resistance to change.**" She waited.

All three of the guests sat thinking for a moment. The silence was deafening.

Charley Carz broke the silence. "Let's get on with it. I'm happy you called this meeting and I want to hear more."

Both of the other guests nodded their assent.

Wanta and Stew began explaining in detail the conversation they had had several nights earlier. Stew elaborated on his dream and how it had affected him. Wanta told of the slow down at The Excuse Factory, how The Whinery had been financially supporting them. Stew jumped in and spoke of the impact of the slow down at the N & S Railroad, and how there was not enough work to justify keeping all of their employees.

Now came the difficult part to explain. Squelchonians always waited until the very last moment to make any changes. Even then, they fought against change vociferously. "If we wait to act," Wanta said, "we will not be able to recover. We won't be able to make up for the losses. These problems will destroy Squelch and ruin the lives of almost everyone here."

Right Handed Lefty spoke up. "Seems like either path is going to cause us some pain. If we resist change we will be very uncomfortable, and if we do change we will be very uncomfortable. However, if we learn to change, our discomfort will end at some point. If we don't, it could last forever. So, what choice do we have?"

Harriet was the next to speak. "I've always known this day was coming," she said. "It was obvious to me many years ago that this culture of ours could not endure forever. It was self-defeating. I have never said anything to anyone about it until this very moment. I, for one, am glad about the small ray of hope. I think everyone will be glad when they lose their fear of learning."

Charley, who had been deep in thought, was the last to speak. "I'm sick of old cars," he said. "I thought I was a Squelcher, but more and more these past couple of years, I have started feeling different than the others around here. I, too, have never said a word about the way I feel, but recently, it has been difficult for me to stop thinking Squirmy thoughts. I thought something was wrong with me. Now I know that's not true."

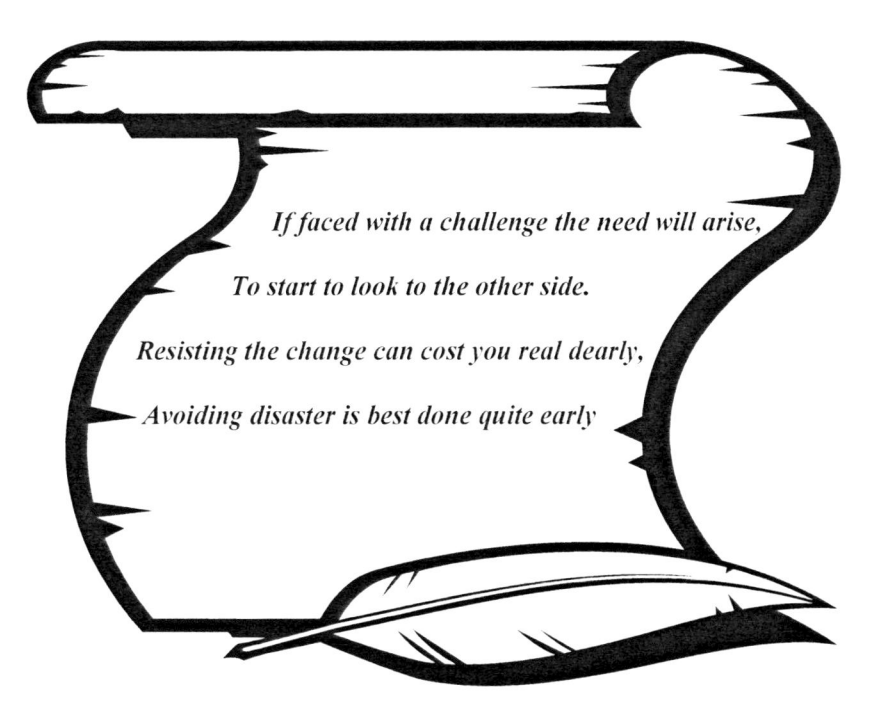

If faced with a challenge the need will arise,

To start to look to the other side.

Resisting the change can cost you real dearly,

Avoiding disaster is best done quite early

Both Wanta and Stew were feeling more comfortable by now. They both realized how many kindred spirits they had found, and began wondering how many more there were in the town of Squelch.

That's when Harriet spoke up. "I know there are many more people like us here in Squelch. There have to be."

"There are," Wanta said. "That small ray of hope is the product of positive thinking. It did not show up by accident. It was certainly the result of more than the mere handful of people here in this room." Wanta felt more energized than she had in decades. "I think that all of us have that quest to learn. The leaders of this town have done everything to create a negative environment and stifle learning, but it cannot be stopped."

"Here's what I know without a doubt," Wanta continued. "All human beings are born with the ability to learn. If you think about it, you have to learn not to learn. Stopping the learning process is actually learning. The energy is misdirected. The most anti-learning Squelchonian can be turned around. Squelchers weren't born that way, and they don't have to stay that way." Wanta watched the faces of the others. Most were deeply engaged in thought, and what pleasure she found in that. It had been years since she had seen anything like it. Even more delightful was how receptive everyone was at the thought of learning and change. *I'm a Squinch no more!* she thought to herself. *Life is great!*

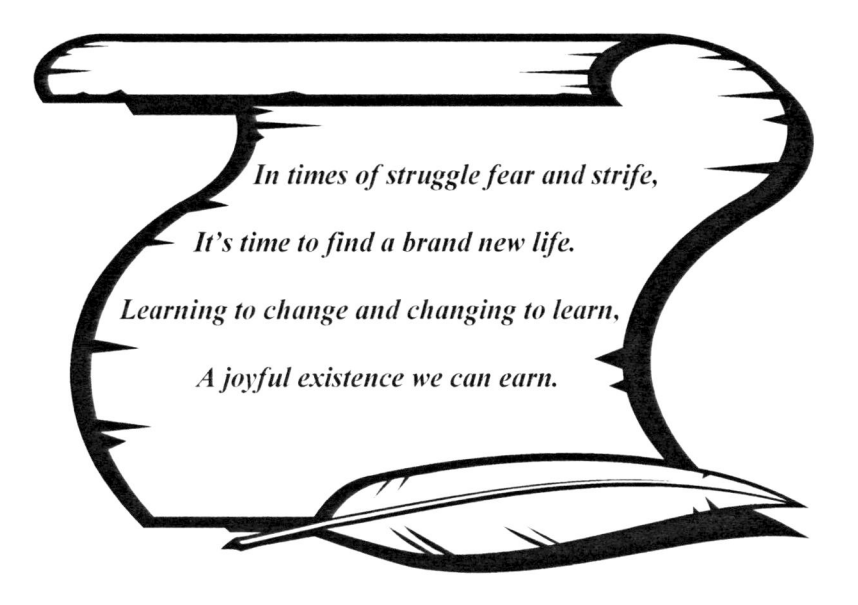

> *In times of struggle fear and strife,*
>
> *It's time to find a brand new life.*
>
> *Learning to change and changing to learn,*
>
> *A joyful existence we can earn.*

Life in Squelch was about to be dramatically altered. But it would require careful thinking and planning. Everyone agreed to meet again in two days to decide on a course of action that would turn things around in Squelch. They knew that just getting started was the hardest part. But once they did, they would create a force that would be impossible to stop.

As they were saying their goodbyes in the front yard, Stew casually looked up. He became excited. "Look," he said, pointing upward. "Can you believe it? The small ray of hope is bigger. I think we've started something."

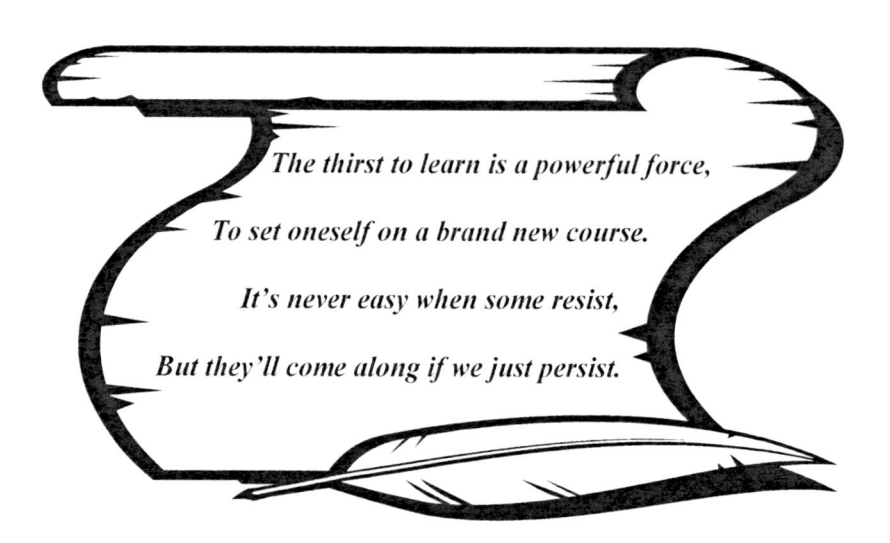

The thirst to learn is a powerful force,

To set oneself on a brand new course.

It's never easy when some resist,

But they'll come along if we just persist.

Chapter Twelve:
Stew Starts to Stew

Everyone who attended the Wiggle's meeting felt like a new person, as though they had a new lease on life. Each one was anticipating the next meeting with a fervor that had lain dormant for many years.

Two days later, as they gathered together again in the home of Wanta and Stew, each person was eager to share their ideas with the others.

Stew started by saying, "I for one am ready to learn. I have spent every waking moment thinking about learning since our last meeting, and I haven't felt better in years. I know we are on the right path."

Each shared similar thoughts as they elaborated on what they had been doing and thinking since their last meeting.

Stew and the others listed the names of possible candidates in Squelch who might have a vested interest their cause, and by the end of the meeting, they had a list of several hundred individuals who would more than likely be eager to join them in the fight for the survival of their town.

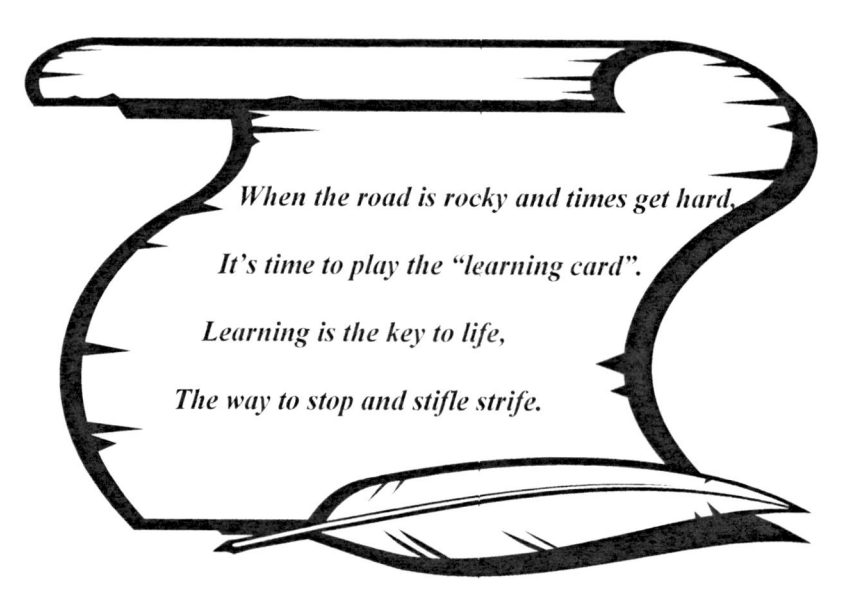

> *When the road is rocky and times get hard,*
>
> *It's time to play the "learning card".*
>
> *Learning is the key to life,*
>
> *The way to stop and stifle strife.*

Wanta addressed the group, "If we are to turn this town around, we've got to get out of the excuse business. There's no market for excuses anymore. What I'm stuck on is what we'll produce if we can't make excuses anymore. We've got to have something else, and right now, I don't know what that could be. We need some ideas. Any thoughts?"

They all seemed lost. Everyone agreed that they couldn't make excuses anymore; that was self-evident; so they began freewheeling, throwing ideas out. As they did, Wanta was amazed to see how uncritical everyone was being. They were actually having fun, laughing and joking, and even though some of the ideas were quite bad, no one scoffed at them.

Stew threw forth an idea that made everyone silent. "I remember hearing something that Squirmonians do," he said. "They, as you recall, have historically been known as learners. To capture their lessons, they create Squimmericks. Maybe some of you have heard of them. They have hundreds, thousands of them, stockpiled in a warehouse in Squirm. To the best of my knowledge, they just keep them there, collecting dust. What if instead of marketing excuses, we marketed Squimmericks? There's got to be a huge market for them, undoubtedly bigger than the market for excuses. We could go into the learning business instead of the excuse business."

Wanta's heart swelled with pride and at ingenuity of her husband. In less than a week he had changed from Squelcher to Squincher. It was only a matter of time before both of them would be Squirmers. She was remorseful about how long they had spent being Squelchers, but in her typically positive way, saw the future brightly before them.

"Wow, what a great idea," said Charley. "Selling Squimmericks that empower people to learn. That would be an incredible product to deliver to the world."

Harriet began laughing loudly. "You know what's so funny?" she asked. "If we do this, we might actually out-squirm Squirm. Now that's a hoot!"

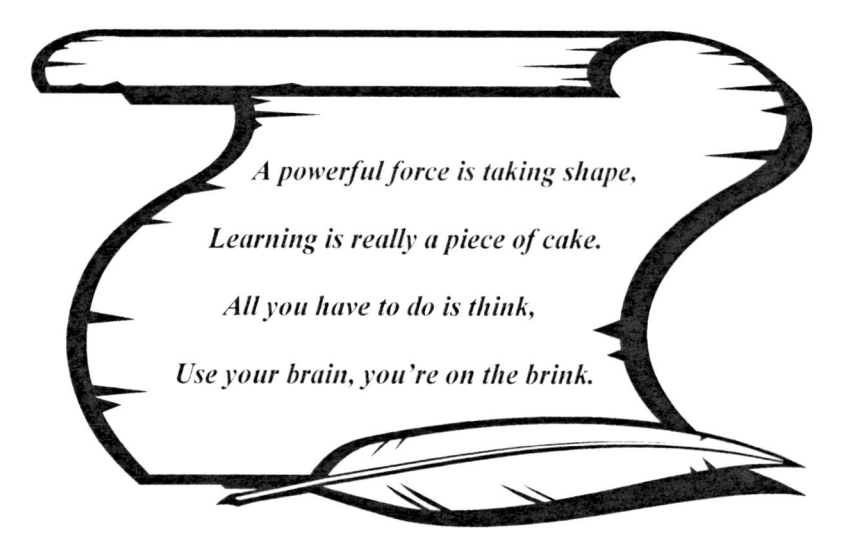

A powerful force is taking shape,

Learning is really a piece of cake.

All you have to do is think,

Use your brain, you're on the brink.

"Yeah," said Right Handed Lefty. "How could they have missed this one? They've got a goldmine sitting right in their own backyard. This is a winner!"

"We've got to approach them about a partnership," Wanta said. "What I know about Squirmonians is that they will do anything and everything to encourage learning. I think they'll be open to working with us to develop the worldwide market for Squimmericks...maybe even a catalog or retail store where people can buy Squimmericks and we could call the store Squimmerickessories. It will help them keep their poems fresh, and we can help them create new ones. It seems such a waste to leave them lying in a warehouse when the world is so ready for them." Wanta's mind was racing. This was the idea that would put Squelch on the map, and move them back into the world of learning.

"How will we approach them?" Harriet said. She loved the idea. In fact, she thought she might even be able to create an entire line of clothing using lines of Squimmericks. The name "Squimtogs" kept popping into her mind.

"I have several friends in Squirm, and I could broach the subject with them," said Wanta. "They are friends with Professor Squirm and could arrange a meeting with him. Just say the word and I'll make some phone calls and set it up. Are we in agreement?"

Everyone agreed.

"It's such a great idea," Stew said, "that now I'm worried that they won't like it or won't agree to it. What if they say no?"

Wanta encouraged him. "Squirmonians, wherever you find them, are always open to new ideas and innovations; this much I know. I can't for a moment believe that they would be anything but open to our idea. I also think they would be delighted to know how we've come full circle."

"Then we're agreed," Stew said. "You are going to meet with Professor Squirm, and we're going to be in the Squimmerick business."

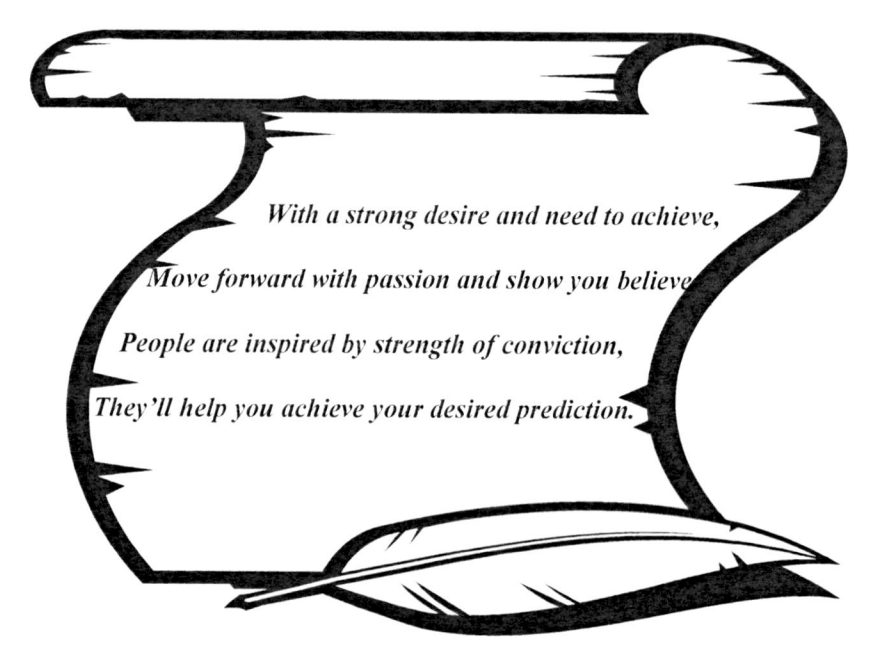

> *With a strong desire and need to achieve,*
> *Move forward with passion and show you believe,*
> *People are inspired by strength of conviction,*
> *They'll help you achieve your desired prediction.*

The path was now decided. As they ended their meeting, Stew again showed his Squirmacious side. "When we go into the Squimmerick business," he asked, "what are we going to call our town? Squelch won't fit anymore."

Wanta quickly replied, "I have been wondering about that myself. Let's save that topic until after the meeting with Professor Squirm. There's a tremendous synergy among all of us, and I have no doubt we'll be able to find the name that fits."

It was agreed, and they adjourned. Once again, as the group departed the Wiggles' residence, they noticed the small ray of hope was even larger. Attitudes were changing, and the ever-growing ray of hope was the evidence of that fact.

Chapter Thirteen:
Wanta and the Professor

Wanta sat facing Professor Squirm. She was barely able to contain her excitement. Quickly gathering her thoughts, she began explaining the dilemma that faced Squelch -- the dire straights they were in and the ideas that she and her group had discussed as a means of addressing the problem.

Kind Professor Squirm listened to her intently as she detailed their ideas and plans. She was fearful that he might say, "I told you so," but soon came to realize that a true Squirmonian never thought that way. He showed eagerness to help and willingness to listen -- the kind of high-level encouragement Wanta had hoped to receive.

Professor Squirm was delighted with Wanta's proposal. "I've always known that the best of you folks would rise to the top. You know we've always wished you the best, and we're willing to help if we could, if you wanted the help. I am so pleased that you've come today. What you've proposed is an outstanding idea, and the people of Squirm and myself are ready to help. I know you've got some rough days ahead of you.

Learning and change is never the easiest path, but it is the most rewarding. Consider our partnership officially formed as of now. Let's work together to help one another in our mutual endeavor of taking our Squimmericks to the world. When do you want to start?"

Wanta was touched by Professor Squirm's willingness to help, his openness to her ideas, and his sincerity. The systematic approach and speed with which he made his decision was surprising to her, considering how decisions were always belabored and avoided in her town. She didn't want to dote on the Professor, but her admiration showed.

Professor Squirm said, "I don't know why we never thought of this. I guess sometimes we become so accustomed to doing things a certain way, even in a town like Squirm, that we miss the obvious. It's always refreshing to get a new idea from someone outside, an idea that wakes you up and gets you learning again. Thank you. You've reminded me -- all of us -- of the power of synergistic thinking. When minds work together, there's no limit to the possibilities. I know that we've helped you; but I want you to know, you've helped us too. This will sharpen all of us, and I've no doubt, you'll help us keep Squirming. This is a great lesson for all of us."

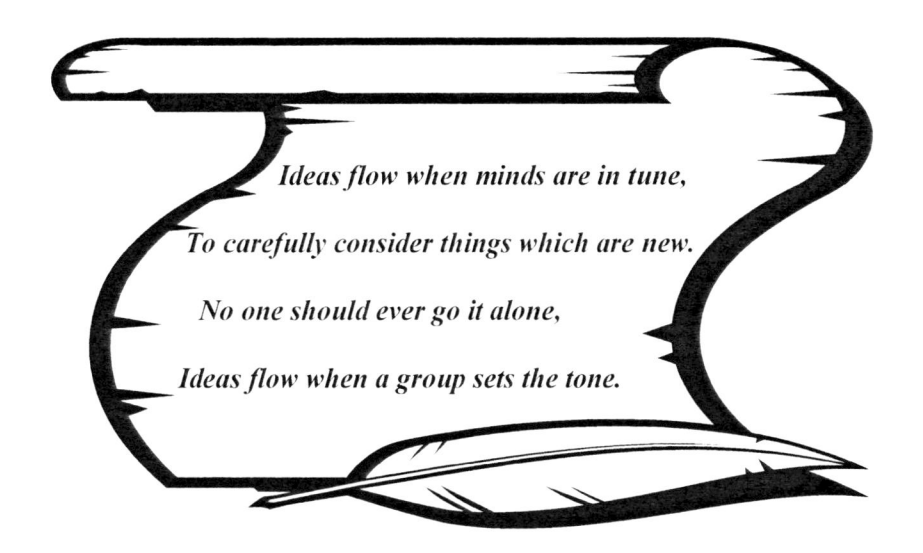

> *Ideas flow when minds are in tune,*
>
> *To carefully consider things which are new.*
>
> *No one should ever go it alone,*
>
> *Ideas flow when a group sets the tone.*

Wanta couldn't wait to return to Squelch and share the good news with her colleagues. No longer making excuses, the citizens of Squelch had bright days ahead. She knew they would be filled with challenges, and there would be frustrating moments. But, after all, isn't that what happens when you're learning?

When you're learning, you're Squirming. And when you're Squirmming, your resistance breaks down. Wanta Wiggle began to realize in fact, that her very own name implied, a desire to learn and be more successful – Wanta Wiggled to Squirm…SQUIRM ON!

Chapter Fourteen:
Making It Happen!

Andy sat in rapt attention as J. T. finished his tale of Squirm. It was impossible not to notice how passionately he felt about this topic of Learning and how he dearly loved telling this fable.

"So, what happened?" Andy inquired.

"What do you think happened?" J. T. responded. "Why don't you finish the story?"

"Well, as I see it, once the town of Squelch got out of the business of making excuses, they began a new path of Squirming. They did it by taking the obvious and turning it into something very special. Squimmericks were a hot item, and all of a sudden they became innovative enough to see that. They started learning. Guess they had never forgotten their ability to learn, it had just gone dormant."

"Sounds like a happy ending to me," J. T. replied. "You see, the Squelchonians got so caught up in perpetuating their mistaken beliefs that it became their way of life. No amount of logic or convincing could change that. What did change their attitudes was their innate need to learn because their survival depended on it. It took a powerful stimulus to cause that to happen, and then there was no stopping it."

Andy understood. "I now see why The Company has stood out so splendidly throughout the years. You never allowed people to rest on their laurels. We were always searching, you made sure of that. Often, we did not even know what it was that we were searching for, but we searched nonetheless."

"That's right, Andy. If you think you know what you are searching for, it immediately limits your field of vision. You just have to constantly be learning, and when you are, you find yourself constantly searching. Without the learning, new ideas, new concepts, new opportunities would pass you by. You wouldn't even notice them, and even on the outside chance that you did, you wouldn't be able to seize those opportunities even if you did recognize them. There's something very positive to be said about readiness."

Andy really understood, now more than ever the personal struggle he had been experiencing. He had not recognized what had caused him to want to stay in his comfort zone. What's more, J. T.'s gentle demeanor, coupled with his basic understanding of human nature, made him feel that it was nothing about which he should be ashamed.

He should only feel shame if he chose to do nothing about it.

J. T. wanted to make another important point. "I wanted you to join The Company because I believed that you could be a great leader. I know, you were a good Manager, but Managers are not what we need. Leaders never blame, they participate, and they take responsibility. Leadership is about setting an example, not accusing and pointing fingers. Learning is something for which each of us must take personal responsibility, no matter what our title. If the leaders of The Company won't do it, it is unreasonable to expect our colleagues will either. We, the leaders, create the environment."

"Managers command, Andy, leaders inspire."

"Don't you need to be able to be both?", Andy wondered.

"Absolutely. Sometimes acting as a manager is the appropriate strategy; however, even when commanding, if you cannot inspire others to feel the commitment and passion about what you want them to do, mediocrity will be the result."

"One of the reasons I so wanted to be a part of The Company, is because of that leadership," Andy told J. T. "The people that make up The Company have an outstanding reputation. It has always amazed me how envious others are of what has been and continues to be accomplished here."

J. T. knew that of which Andy was referring. "We have a waiting list of people who want to become Company colleagues. We rarely have to recruit. They find us. Do you know why?"

"Well, I think so," Andy said. "We're about the finest place in the world to work. I know that's a big part of it."

"That's true," J. T. agreed, "but it didn't just happen. I realized a long time ago that the environment of a workplace is everything. The environment creates the climate where people must function. A dysfunctional environment breeds dysfunctional behavior in employees, and that serves no one. Our customers and our stakeholders would pay the ultimate price for that."

In his business classes in college and in his postgraduate work, Andy learned little about the topic that J. T. was explaining. Sure, he knew about efficiency, revenues, spreadsheets, and profit and loss statements, all of the ways to measure business results. However, when it came to the real place in an organization where business results are actually achieved, almost no effort was expended in that arena. The *people part* of business education seemed to be sorely lacking.

"It all comes down to people. The results any organization creates is in the hands of its people, pure and simple." J. T. lightly pounded on his desk as he made this point. He wanted to make sure Andy got it. "The people, however, function within their environment to create those results. The job of a leader is to create the environment where optimum results can be achieved."

Andy got it! He intuitively knew it but now, it was really beginning to gel. As he reflected on his past behavior with his team in The Company, he felt slightly ashamed. This great man had trusted him with his most precious business asset, his people. Andy had not, in his personal opinion, deserved that asset. He shifted in his chair, experiencing some real discomfort. He wished he could start with The Company all over again. Trying to stifle that notion, it suddenly dawned on him that maybe he could, at least attitudinally.

"People do what they have to do to either thrive in their environment, because that's the expectation, or to survive because that could also be the expectation. In any event, it is the environment of the organization that most often dictates that attitude. It is the leader's job to create the right environment."

Andy asked, "How do I reconcile this with my business school training. I really never learned this, stuff. In fact I don't ever recall even discussing it. How do I learn this? Where do I learn this?"

"It has been right in front of you since you joined The Company. You were too busy to learn. You were so busy 'managing' you didn't have time to learn to lead. But, if you want to accomplish your personal vision, you will have to become a leader."

"Andy, listen to your people, listen to whom they serve. Tune in to them. When leaders start giving their people responsibility for their productivity, they usually step up and become accountable. If they don't, and sometimes that happens, then they need to go somewhere that will enable them to conduct their work in a more control-oriented environment. In any event, those folks are just not suited for our culture and often they figure it out and bow out gracefully. They're not bad people, just a bad fit."

"This is so obvious. How could I have not understood all this?" Andy asked, mostly talking out loud to himself.

"I know." J. T. continued. "You see, Andy, anyone could have accomplished what we have accomplished here at The Company, and I mean that sincerely. There is really no magic to it. The problem is, they imprison their people with structure, and bureaucracy, and then egos start getting in the way. Before you know it, they've not only lost sight of their main vision and mission, but their values become completely compromised. Ultimately, their people pay the price. Sure their profits look good, temporarily, but how do you sustain great business results when you eliminate the talent you need to achieve those results? The simple answer is, YOU DON'T. You hit the wall, and then what? Those quick-fix artists and one-song bands leave little but problems in their wake once they depart. And they always depart."

"The company winds up being a shell of its former self. The morale is in the tank, great people leave, and with them great ideas. This is the ultimate Squelch. Instead of using innovation, ingenuity and knowledge to Squirm; they Squelch and Stifle and thus kill the spirits of the people upon which they rely upon to have a great company that produces great results. Business requires great patience. Instant gratification should be sought elsewhere."

"Don't the leaders have a responsibility to the shareholders?" Andy wanted to know. "I get somewhat torn as I think about this. Where should loyalties lie?"

"It does the shareholders no good if the leaders of an organization destroy it for the sake of a few cent dividend. People are the ultimate key to profits anyway, and if the people in a company are suffering you can bet the profits are as well. Taking the short sighted view, getting rid of people is the easy way out, but maybe the most irresponsible as well."

"Don't you think that a great strategy is necessary to create a great business?" Andy wondered.

"Absolutely," J. T. explained, "but which comes first, the strategy or the people? That's the age-old argument, a chicken and egg argument. My observation of great businesses is that they start with great people, the right people. They'll help build the strategy. After all, they are responsible for implementing that strategy. The graveyard is full of 'Titanic-Type' disasters where the reverse was attempted."

"That top-down approach might work in the short term but is seldom sustaining."

Andy was puzzled. "It sounds to me like a real hands-off approach to business. Isn't that also a formula for disaster?"

"You bet it is," J. T. was quick to respond. "This is not hands-off. This is hands on, *very* hands on. If the manager became a leader, then he plays the role of a facilitator. The problem is, a leader's ego can start taking over. They want control; they want to claim credit. In so doing, they rob their people of their sense of accomplishment. But, that's flawed thinking."

"If a leader would understand that he or she will ultimately be judged by the results of his team, he could then help that team gain credit for its accomplishments. That's a huge morale booster. When morale goes up, so does productivity and the sense that one is responsible for his or her business results. That's how you achieve high levels of accountability."

"It would seem to me that too much freedom is also one of those things that can create anarchy within an organization. Don't you think that handing over the reins to just anyone is bad business?" Andy seemed confused, but was trying desperately to grasp what J. T. was saying.

"You can't just hand over the reins to anyone. Above all, you must have the right people. Without them, you cannot achieve great business results, much less give them the freedom they might want." J. T. knew that Andy was struggling so he slowed down as he continued. "Freedom is something we all value. In fact, we will fight to get it and fight to keep it. But you must realize that no highly functioning business --- or society for that matter – has ever survived long without it."

"However, Andy, freedom comes with responsibility-- Responsibility for one's own actions. People who will not accept personal responsibility ultimately relinquish their rights to the freedom they desire. They must realize that they cannot have it both ways."

Andy was experiencing a bit of turmoil as was evidenced by his physical uneasiness. He was frowning, fidgeting in his chair and seemed a bit disturbed.

"Andy," J. T. smiled, "I can see your uneasiness. How absolutely splendid. You, my friend, are now Squirming. I can see it. Welcome to The Company. I think you're finally on board, and I think our meeting is over."

Mirror, mirror
in the book,
Do I dare to
take a look.
If I look what
will I see,
A Squirm
or Squelch,
it's up to me!

photo by Mike Simons

Squirmologist Author & Leadership Team:
(l-r) Dr. Jeffrey Magee, PDM/CSP/CMC,
Ginny Simons, and Dave Simons

For More Information Contact
www.SquirmToLearn.com
… OR …

Dave & Ginny Simons at:
THE PERFORMANCE RESOURCE GROUP
6660 S. Sheridan, Ste. 120
Tulsa, OK, 74133
Toll free 1-800-582-0082
www.PerformanceResourceGroup.com

Jeffrey Magee, Ph.D., PDM, CSP, CMC at:
JEFF MAGEE INTERNATIONAL/JMI, Inc.
POB 701918
Tulsa, OK, 74170-1918
Toll free 1-877-90-MAGEE
www.JeffreyMagee.com/library.asp

$$C = \left(\frac{T + A + P}{E^2}\right) = R$$

Training (past + future)

Capability   Results

A = Attitude

P = Performance

E = Expectations (them + me)

Names — Networking Adv.

#1 Mktg.   Qualified Prospects   25%

#2 Selling   (Rec.) Prospects   25%

#3 Admin.   25%

New Members

Profile Chapter Members